Great Men
OF THE
BIBLE

A GUIDE FOR GUYS

Martin Pable, OFM Cap

GREAT MEN OF THE BIBLE
A Guide for Guys
by Martin Pable, OFM Cap

Cover art and interior illustrations from Bigstock
Editing by Gregory F. Augustine Pierce
Design and typesetting by Patricia A. Lynch

Copyright © 2014 by Martin Pable, OFM Cap

Published by In Extenso Press
Distributed exclusively by ACTA Publications, 4848 N. Clark Street,
Chicago, IL 60640, (800) 397-2282, www.actapublications.com

Scripture texts in this work are taken from *The Message: The Bible in
Contemporary Language (Catholic/Ecumenical Edition)*, © 2013 by Eugene
Peterson. Used with permission of NavPress.

Library of Congress Catalog Number: 2014913305
ISBN: 978-0-87946-995-5
Printed in the United States of America by Total Printing Systems
Year 25 24 23 22 21 20 19 18 17 16 15 14
Printing 12 11 10 9 8 7 6 5 4 3 2

♻ Text printed on 30% post-consumer recycled paper

CONTENTS

Introduction • 5

Abraham • 7

Jacob • 21

Joseph • 37

Moses • 55

David •81

Elijah • 95

Jeremiah • 107

John the Baptist • 125

Joseph of Nazareth • 137

Peter • 153

Paul • 173

Epilogue • 207

INTRODUCTION

This One's for You, Guys

Men. We are spiritual beings, just as women are. But masculine spirituality is in many ways different from feminine spirituality. It is rougher, less pious, more oriented to our work, more concerned with function than form. And it needs male role models.

Recently, I have been conducting a series of programs for men entitled "Great Men of the Bible." As the men shared their reflections in small groups I have been touched by the ways they connected the Biblical stories about men with their own experiences as men striving to live spiritually in an increasingly secularized world.

Another push to write this book came from a talk I heard on "Using the Media to Tell Our Story." One of the presenter's statements that struck me forcefully was his claim that "whoever tells the stories shapes the culture." It is not difficult to grasp the truth behind that statement: namely, stories (whether true or fictional) can be far more powerful than logical arguments for shaping people's beliefs and attitudes. Think of the great stories in literature—in legends, history books, movies, stage plays, and popular songs. Whether it is consciously or not, people's values are strongly influenced by encounters with these stories.

In my mind, some of the most fascinating stories about men are those found in the Hebrew and Christian Scriptures. Not only are they filled with human drama, tragedy, and heroism, but they reveal profound truths about human beings and their relationships with God and one another. Moreover, they provide insights into the great questions of human existence: What is the good life? What is the purpose of our existence? What is our final destiny? How ought we to treat one another? Indeed: "Whoever tells the stories shapes the culture."

I was also pleased to be introduced recently to *The Message* by Eugene Peterson, a contemporary paraphrasal translation of the complete Bible from the ancient languages into modern, idiomatic, American English. I thought to myself, "This translation makes the Scriptures come alive in ways that I have never experienced before. I think the men I know would be interested in reading it." So I have used it exclusively throughout the book. Readers will find it interesting to compare the translation with that of their own Bible.

Maybe women will be interested in this book as well. I hope so. There are similar books about great women in the Bible that men should certainly read. But this one is aimed at my fellow men. Guys, this one's for you. Please join me in examining these stories of great men of the Bible for their human and spiritual wisdom.

Martin Pable, OFM Cap.
Milwaukee, Wisconsin

ABRAHAM

(Flawed) Father of Our Faith

Abraham, whom both the Bible and the liturgy call "the father of our faith," is honored and revered by all three religions of the Book—Judaism, Christianity, and Islam. His story is one of heroic fidelity to God, as well as of human weakness and failure.

The Book of Genesis tells us that Abraham's father was a man named Terah, who was said to be a descendant of Noah's son Shem. Terah lived in a place called "Ur of the Chaldeans," an extremely ancient city located in present-day southern Iraq. "Chaldea," however, is an anachronism, since this nation was not known until about a thousand years after Abraham's time. Also, his original name—Abram—was later changed by God.

As with many families in those times, Terah sought better land for his crops and herds. He decided to migrate north and west to the land of Canaan, taking Abram; Abram's wife, Sarai; and his grandson Lot with him. But before reaching Canaan, he decided to settle in Haran, near present-day Syria, where he died.

Sometime later, Abram received his first revelation from God:

"Leave your country, your family, and your father's home
for a land that I will show you.
I'll make you a great nation
and bless you.
I'll make you famous;
you'll be a blessing...

All the families of the Earth
   will be blessed through you."

                                          Genesis 12: 1, 3

The Bible does not record Abram's internal reaction to this religious experience of his vocation or calling. We do not even know if he had received any knowledge or instruction about the God of his ancestors, the descendants of Noah. The text simply says, "So Abram left just as God said, and Lot (his nephew) left with him (Genesis 1:4).

I believe many men have had experiences like this. Not that we heard a voice or saw a vision, but something deep inside spoke to our mind or heart, and we were faced with a decision: "Should I follow this inspiration or ignore it? Maybe I just ate too much garlic last night." Yet something about the challenge was compelling, and we found ourselves saying, "I need to do this, regardless of the risk or uncertainty." Notice that the original motivation was economic: Terah sought better land for his crops and herds. Many men make decisions based on being better able to provide for their family. Notice also that "Lot left with him." This is another experience men have. A lot of our decisions affect others, including our immediate and extended family members.

God again appeared to Abram and said, "I will give this land to your children" (Genesis 12:7).

This must have seemed ludicrous to Abram because he was a migrant in a land that was already occupied by various ethnic tribes collectively called "Canaanites." Besides, Abram and his wife, Sarai (later changed by God to Sarah), had no children at the time. Yet God was now making a promise to Abram, and, once again, he believed. In fact, he gave a religious response: "He built an altar there and prayed to GOD" (Genesis 12:8).

How often do we men dream the impossible dream and then come to believe we can do it? And isn't our response often a spiritual one: to thank God for giving us a mission worthy of our life? And isn't optimism a better way to live than being pessimistic?

Abraham was complicated—like we are

As so often happens, however, even good people betray their own values under stress. When a severe famine overtook the land of Canaan, Abram and Sarai migrated south to the land of Egypt. Abram was aware of the warped cultural practice of the pharaohs of Egypt. For example, when an attractive married woman would catch the eye of the pharaoh, the husband would be killed, and the wife would be forced into the pharaoh's harem. Knowing this, Abram tells Sarai: "Look. We both know that you're a beautiful woman. When the Egyptians see you they're going to say, 'Aha! That's his wife!' and kill me. But they'll let you live. Do me a favor. Tell them you're my sister. Because of you, they'll welcome me and let me live" (Genesis 12:11-13).

Men have to make these kinds of tactical decisions all the time. Do we stand and fight an evil, even if it means almost certain disaster, or do we fudge the truth or look away in order to live to fight another day? Besides, Abram's lie was not a complete lie but a half-truth; in his culture, any female relative (including wife) was called "a sister." So indeed, Abram's life was spared, but Sarai was still taken into the Pharaoh's harem. Many say Abram was a coward. He was. So are we sometimes. But there was more to the story.

> Because of her, Abram got along very well: he accumulated sheep and cattle, male and female donkeys, men and women servants, and camels. But GOD hit Pharaoh hard because of Abram's wife Sarai; everybody in the palace got seriously sick.
>
> Pharaoh called for Abram, "What's this that you've done to me? Why didn't you tell me that she's your wife? Why did you say, 'She's my sister' so that I'd take her as my wife? Here's your wife back—take her and get out!"
>
> Pharaoh ordered his men to get Abram out of the country. They sent him and his wife and everything he owned on their way.
>
> Genesis 12:16-20

So, there we have it. Men know that sometimes our weakness or cowardice or even sin works out for us in the end. What are we supposed to do with that reality? We have to forgive ourselves, move on, and somehow try to understand that God works in very hard-to-comprehend ways.

When Abram and Sarai returned to the land of Canaan, another conflict ensued. Since there was plenty of unclaimed grazing land, both Abram and his nephew Lot were able to increase their flocks and herds. Soon the two men began to quarrel over the grazing rights. Abram dealt with the conflict in a very clever manner. He told Lot: "Let's not have fighting between us, between your shepherds and my shepherds. After all, we're family. Look around. Isn't there plenty of land out there? Let's separate. If you go left, I'll go right; if you go right, I'll go left" (Genesis 13: 8-9).

Our weakness or cowardice or even sin works out for us in the end.

And his generosity was rewarded. After Lot separated from him, God said to Abram: "Open your eyes, look around. Look north, south, east, and west. Everything you see, the whole land spread out before you, I will give to you and your children forever. I'll make your descendants like dust—counting your descendants will be as impossible as counting the dust of the Earth. So—on your feet, get moving! Walk through the country, its length and breadth; I'm giving it all to you" Genesis 13:8-9, 14-15.

No doubt many of us can remember times in our own lives when we chose to sacrifice our own interest or preference in order to help a family member or friend in need. Difficult as it was, we experienced some gift or blessing from God in return. I recall a situation from my own life. I was based in Milwaukee for 13 years and enjoying success in my ministry of teaching, counseling, and speaking to various parish groups. One day my superiors called me in and asked me to take a different assignment: director of our novitiate program in Huntington, Indiana. They said I could turn it down if I felt that was best, but they asked me to seriously consider it because the need was great. At first I resisted the idea strongly. I was happy where I was; I didn't want to leave my comfort zone for a totally new assignment in a small town far from my roots and my friends. But then I recalled that I have taken a vow of obedience. This was a reasonable request from my superiors and I had no solid reason to turn it down. So I said Yes, and felt a deep sense of peace. And, very much like Abraham, God blessed me abundantly. Maybe you have had a similar experience.

Abram doubted God—just as we all do

Chapter 15 of Genesis begins: "After all these things, this word of GOD came to Abram in a vision: 'Don't be afraid, Abram. I'm your shield. Your reward will be grand!' Abram said, 'GOD, Master, what use are your gifts as long as I'm childless and Eliezer of Damascus is going to inherit everything?' Abram continued, 'See, you've given me no children, and now a mere house servant is going to get it all'" (Genesis 15:1-3).

Abram is legitimately distressed. God had promised to make him the father of many nations, yet he and Sarai have not been able to conceive even one child. The situation seems hopeless. Haven't we all been there in our lives? But God doubles down on his promise: "Look at the sky. Count the stars. Can you do it? Count your descendants! You're going to have a big family, Abram!" (Genesis 15:5).

Don't we men do that too? When things aren't going well, don't we double down and try harder? Don't we expect (or at least pray) God will help us succeed? So that's what Abram did: "And he believed! Believed GOD! God declared him 'Set-Right-with-God'" (Genesis 15:6).

Abram put his faith in the Lord, yes. But at the same time, he asks God for some kind of sign to strengthen his faith. So, God asks him to set up the covenant ritual. This was familiar to many tribal societies at the time. When one chief wanted to make an alliance (covenant) with another tribal chief, they would take a couple of animals and large birds, split them in half, and mount each half on poles facing each other, with some space in between. Then the two chiefs would walk between the carcasses and lock arms in the center, gaze at the animals, and say, "May the same thing happen to me if I violate this covenant!" Pretty strong, earthy stuff.

So Abram sets up the poles and carcasses, walks between them—and waits. But God makes no appearance. Meanwhile, vultures are sweeping down and picking at the carcasses, and Abram has to fight them off. Now it's getting dark, and just before sunset "a trance fell on Abram, and a deep, terrifying darkness enveloped him" (Genesis 1:12). Then God speaks to Abram and warns him that his descendants will have to suffer much and wait a long time until the covenant is fulfilled:

> GOD said to Abram, "Know this: your descendants will live as outsiders in a land not theirs; they'll be enslaved and beaten down for 400 years. Then I'll punish their slave masters; your offspring will march out of there loaded with plunder. But not you; you'll have a long and full life and die a good and peaceful death."
>
> *Genesis 15:13-14*

Suddenly a flaming torch passed between the carcasses, and Abram knew this was the sign of God's presence, promising to keep his part of the covenant. He stood up greatly strengthened and encouraged.

All of us have had experiences of doubting God's promises, even the divine presence in our lives. Sometimes I refer to this as "spiritual depression." We need not be ashamed of this. After all, God does not usually speak to us or appear to us visibly. "We walk by faith and not by sight," as one of our liturgical songs says. It's at those times that we are called, like Abram, to keep fighting off the feelings of doubt, discouragement, and weariness that can overtake us.

Sometimes it helps to talk to someone about our feelings: spouse, friend, priest or deacon, or prayer group. And sometimes, all we can do is wait, like Abram, until we experience God's presence and encouragement and believe. Only then are we "set-right-with-God." It is all part of the spiritual journey.

Abraham tries to take things in his own hands— just as we do

Months and years were passing, and Abram and Sarai still had no children. What has happened to God's promise to make us founders of a great nation, they must have wondered. Rather than wait on God's time, they decided to take matters into their own hands. Sarai had a maidservant named Hagar. One day she said to Abram: Have intercourse with my maid; perhaps she will be able to give us children. "Abram agreed to do what Sarai said," the Bible reports wryly, in what must be one of its more humorous verses (Genesis, 16:2).

Now, before we judge the couple, we need to recall that their action would not have been considered immoral according to the customs of those times. Continuing the family line and name was such a high priority that having children by a servant was an accepted practice. When Hagar became pregnant, taunting Sarai about her sterility, Sarai demanded that Abram punish her. Abram, however, left that up to his wife, who then began to abuse Hagar so badly that Hagar ran away into the wilderness. But an angel of God found her there and told her to return. "You will bear a son," he said, "and you shall call him Ishmael." The name in Hebrew means "God has heard."

> From this pregnancy, you'll get a son: Name him Ishmael;
>   for GOD heard you, GOD answered you.
> He'll be a bucking bronco of a man,
>   a real fighter, fighting and being fought,
> Always stirring up trouble,
>   always at odds with his family.
>
> *Genesis 16:10-12*

We today might see Ishmael as a symbol of some of our modern young males who feel abandoned by their fathers, often becoming wild and anti-social.

As for Abram, the wrongness of his actions was two-fold. First, he tried to solve the childless problem by agreeing with his wife to take matters into his own hands, rather than waiting and trusting in God's promises. Second, he refused to intervene when Sarai and Hagar were quarreling, especially when Sarai began to abuse Hagar.

There are lessons here for us. First, because we males have a strong tendency to fix things when they are not working, we can carry that tendency into human relationships. We fail to understand, however, that sometimes we are powerless to fix or control relationships. After all, we human beings have minds and wills of our own. It is then that we need to rely on the grace and power of God to accomplish what we cannot. We pray and we wait. That is the wisdom of the Quaker prayer-meeting. The group simply sits together in utter silence, quietly asking God to do by his power what they are unable to do.

But sometimes we are called to intervene, to take charge of a situation that is out of control. This is what Abram should have done when the two women in his life were hurting each other. Instead, he remained passive. At times we have a responsibility to step into a dysfunctional or destructive situation, perhaps with the help of others, to solve the problem, "stop the bleeding," and bring about reconciliation and healing.

Abraham makes a covenant with God— just as we must

Chapter 17 of Genesis begins with another appearance of God to Abram. "When Abram was ninety-nine years old, GOD showed up and said to him, 'I am The Strong God, live entirely before me, live to the hilt! I'll make a covenant between us and I'll give you a huge family.' Overwhelmed, Abram fell flat on his face" (Genesis 17:1-3).

Then God changes Abram's name to Abraham and Sarai's to Sarah. Scholars say there is no special significance to the new names, but the fact of the change indicates the importance of these two people for the Hebrew nation:

"This is my covenant with you: You'll be the father of many nations. Your name will no longer be Abram, but Abraham, meaning that 'I'm making you the father of many nations.' I'll make you a father of fathers—I'll make nations from you, kings will issue from you. I'm establishing my covenant between me and you, a covenant that includes your descendants, a covenant that goes on and on and on, a covenant that commits me to be your God and the God of your descendants. And I'm giving you and your descendants this land where you're now just camping, this whole country of Canaan, to own forever. And I'll be their God."

Genesis 17:4-8

As a visible sign of the covenant, God directs that every male be circumcised. This painful and earthy ritual had profound significance for the Hebrew male. It was a wound that symbolically joined the male child to God from the first days of his life. Yes, there was a religious ritual for newborn girls also. The parents would lift her high and offer a prayer of consecration. She too was a child of God and a participant in the covenant with her people.

For the male, however, circumcision was a visible, unmistakable, permanent reminder of who he was: a child/man of God. His sexuality had spiritual significance. This became increasingly important as Jews began to mingle and interact with Gentiles. Every time he looked at his penis, he could remember: I am different; I belong to a spiritual community, dedicated to a unique and transcendent God.

In the New Covenant, circumcision was abolished, and for good reasons. Christians came to realize that Jesus Christ broke down the barriers between Jews and Gentiles, between males and females, between ethnic and racial groups. All people are now called to live in communion with God and with one another. So circumcision was replaced by baptism, a gender-neutral ritual that powerfully symbolizes death to all sin, self-seeking, and all barriers that would divide one race, gender, or class from another. At the same time it symbolizes resurrection to a new life of love in accord with the new commandment of Jesus:

> *This is my command: Love one another the way I loved you. This is the very best way to love. Put your life on the line for your friends. You are my friends when you do the things I command you. I'm no longer calling you servants because servants don't understand what their master is thinking and planning. No, I've named you friends because I've let you in on everything I've heard from the Father.*
>
> *John 15:12-15*

Yet, I think we need to acknowledge that something was lost in abandoning circumcision: the connection between sexuality and spirituality. Wouldn't it be marvelous if we men could stop: a) being ashamed of our penis; and b) making a god out of it? If we could rediscover the sacred connection between the penis and our covenant relationship with God? Perhaps then they could take delight in their sexual power *and* recognize the need for its regulation in harmony with the divine plan. In fact, if we understand the sacrament of baptism deeply enough, it is clear that it is our total person, not just our sexual organs, that is joined to God in the ritual action. All of our body and its functions have sacred significance. There are profound implications here for the way we care for our body, the way we treat one another, and the ways we make love. The dignity of the human body is also the basis for the Church's teachings on reverence for life as well as on the proper use of sexuality.

Abraham passes a test—just as we will

At long last,"GOD visited Sarah exactly as he said he would; GOD did to Sarah what he promised: Sarah became pregnant and gave Abraham a son in his old age, and at the very time God had set. Abraham named him Isaac. When his son was eight days old, Abraham circumcised him just as GOD had commanded" (Genesis 21: 1-4).

Abraham named the boy Isaac, meaning "laughter" in Hebrew. As Sarah said: "God has blessed me with laughter and all who get the news will laugh with me" (Genesis 21: 6). But conflicts arose again between Sarah and her servant, Hagar. Sarah noticed the two boys playing together and demanded that Abraham drive Hagar and her son, Ishmael, out of the house. Abraham did not want to do this, but God assured him it would be all right: "Don't feel badly about the boy and your maid. Do whatever Sarah tells you. Your descendants will come through Isaac. Regarding your maid's son, be assured that I'll also develop a great nation from him—he's your son, too" (Genesis 21:12-13).

We read that God again sent an angel to Hagar in the wilderness and provided her and her son with enough food and water to sustain them until they could settle down. Eventually, Ishmael married a woman from Egypt and his family line continued. In fact, Muslims believe Ishmael to be the founder of Islam, just as Jews claim Isaac.

Next comes the mysterious testing of Abraham. God tells him: "Take your dear son Isaac whom you love and go to the land of Moriah. Sacrifice him there, as a burnt offering on one of the mountains that I'll point out to you" (Genesis 22:2).

The story is full of pathos that pulls on our heart-strings. On the way, the boy notices that they have wood and fire, but no sheep for the sacrifice. Abraham tells him not to worry. God will provide. We can only imagine the agony in the heart of Abraham as he arrives at the mountain, builds the altar, and binds his only son with ropes. Just as he is about to wield the knife, an angel stops him: "Don't lay a hand on that boy! Don't touch him! Now I know how fearlessly you fear God; you didn't hesitate to place your son, your dear son, on the altar for me" (Genesis 22:12). Abraham notices a ram caught by its horns in the bush and offers it as a sacrifice in place of his son. Then God renews the promises to make of Abraham a great nation.

This story often provokes wonderment, even outrage, in people's minds. Why would God require such a severe test of this good man? The Bible itself does not provide a clear answer. Many biblical scholars say the story is probably not historically true, but is a symbolic way of teaching two important truths: 1) we are called to obey and trust God, even when what is being asked of us seems contrary to reason and common sense. Christians throughout history have accepted suffering and even death rather than deny their faith in Christ and his teachings; and 2) at times we may be asked to sacrifice something we worked very hard to achieve because something else has become more important. We might think of some examples: a physician being banned from practice in a hospital because he refuses to perform abortions; a venerable parish church has to close because it can no longer be maintained financially or pastorally. These are heart-rending decisions that call us to respond with obedience to things we do not understand and to trust that "every detail in our lives of love for God is worked into something good" as St. Paul writes (Romans 8:28).

We too will be tested, and we too will be given the means to make the right decisions.

This test tells us we too will be tested, and we too will be given the means to make the right decisions. We just have to look for the angels that are always around us!

Finally, Abraham arranges to find a wife for his son Isaac from among his own kindred back in Haran, because he did not want him to marry a Canaanite woman (see Genesis 24). The story ends with the death and burial of Abraham. He was buried by his sons Isaac and Ishmael, next to his wife Sarah (see Genesis 25:7-11).

So, what do we men learn from this great man of the Bible? We learn that we all have a call from God, that life is difficult, that if we remain faithful—even if we make mistakes—that God will be there for us. Not bad lessons for us to learn.

QUESTIONS FOR REFLECTION AND DISCUSSION

1. Like Abraham, can you think of a time in your life when you embarked on some venture that seemed daunting, but somehow felt right, even God-inspired? What was that like, and what was the outcome?

2. Can you recall a time when you acted generously—even maybe took a loss—but experienced God's blessing?

3. When have you had to wait a long time for God to "show up"? What "birds of prey" threatened to make you give up? How did you fight them off? How did God finally answer?

4. How do you handle it when you try to fix a situation but can't do it? Have there been times when you should have taken action but didn't? Or when you acted too precipitously and should have waited? What happened?

5. Have you ever been asked to give up something you worked hard to gain (like Abraham with Isaac)? How did you decide what God really wanted you to do?

JACOB

Case Study of the Male Journey

After Abraham's son Isaac was married to Rebekah, we read that the couple had twin sons, Esau and Jacob. Esau, who was born first, was named "hairy" because he was a big, striking boy with lots of hair, and Jacob was named "heel" because he came out of the womb grasping the heel of his older brother's foot.

The differences between the two boys as they grew up were striking: "Esau became an expert hunter, an outdoorsman. Jacob was a quiet man preferring life indoors among the tents." (Genesis 25:27) Enjoying cook and hanging around the house, he was his mother's favorite. One day, when Jacob was cooking a stew, Esau came in from the fields famished and asked to have a bowl. Jacob was shrewd:

> Jacob said, "Make me a trade: my stew for your rights as the firstborn." Esau said, "I'm starving! What good is a birthright if I'm dead?"
>
> Jacob said, "First, swear to me." And he did it. On oath Esau traded away his rights as the firstborn. Jacob gave him bread and the stew of lentils. He ate and drank, got up and left. That's how Esau shrugged off his rights as the firstborn.
>
> Genesis 25:34

There are a couple of lessons here for us men today. First, there is more than one way to be a man. Sure we can be outdoorsmen, but we can also be quiet men who prefer "life indoors among the tents." Second, being shrewd (or at least thinking ahead) is not a bad thing. And third, we shouldn't be so quick to abandon our traditions for a "bowl of stew."

Jacob pulls a fast one—just as we do sometimes

Meanwhile, Isaac and Rebekah became quite financially successful, so the birthright that Esau had so cavalierly given to his brother became more valuable. Also, Esau had married two Hittite women, opening the possibility that all their wealth would eventually end up in the hands of people outside the family. Plus, as Genesis says in one of its more humorous passages, their daughters-in-law "turned out to be thorns in the sides of Isaac and Rebekah" (Genesis 26: 35).

Some years pass, and Isaac, who is still partial to the stronger and more-like-his-father, Esau, is growing old and losing his eyesight. One day, he tells Esau to hunt down some wild game and prepare a good stew for him and "bring it to me to eat so that I can give you my personal blessing before I die" (Genesis 27:4). Apparently a father's blessing was different from (and perhaps more possible than) the oldest-son birthright, or maybe Isaac knew nothing about the deal that was made by his two sons many years earlier.

In any case, Rebekah overhears the conversation. She doesn't want her favorite, Jacob, to lose the battle between her boys, so she connives with Jacob. She tells him to get a couple of young goats from the flock, and then cover his arms and neck with the hairy wool. She cooks up a tasty dinner she knows her husband will like, and tells Jacob to bring it to his father, pretending to be Esau.

She gives Jacob some of Esau's outdoor-smelling clothes and sends him in to Isaac with the dinner. Isaac is suspicious at first. He wonders how his elder son found the wild game so quickly. "Because your GOD cleared the way for me" (Genesis 27:20), Jacob answers, but his voice sounds more like Jacob than Esau. When Jacob comes close to his father, Isaac smells the garments of Esau and is convinced. He gives Jacob his blessing and the inheritance promised to the first-born.

He came close and kissed him and Isaac smelled the smell of his clothes. Finally, he blessed him,

> *Ahhh. The smell of my son*
>> *is like the smell of the open country*
>> *blessed by GOD.*
> *May God give you*
>> *of Heaven's dew*
>> *and Earth's bounty of grain and wine.*
> *May peoples serve you*
>> *and nations honor you.*
> *You will master your brothers,*
>> *and your mother's sons will honor you.*
> *Those who curse you will be cursed,*
>> *those who bless you will be blessed.*

Genesis 27:27-29

What are we men to make of this strange story today? That it is okay to lie, cheat, and steal from your brothers? Obviously not. This story was written thousands of years ago in a society with rules much different from ours today. Besides, as Christians we have the advantage of looking back at the Hebrew Scriptures through the lens of the teachings of Jesus.

However, there are some lessons to be learned from the story of Jacob and Esau that apply to us today, or at least give us material to reflect upon.

First and foremost, the entire Old Testament documents how God works through imperfect people, even sinners. God has a plan for the world, and that plan is not brought about solely by the saints among us. In this case, God wanted to form a people out of the descendants of Isaac. Esau, with his foreign wives (who were "thorns in the sides" of his parents), would not have done that. His offspring would have been sucked into the mixed pool of people who were running things at the time. It is significant that Jacob would eventually marry not one, but two full-blooded relatives—Leah and Rachel, daughters of his mother's brother Laban.

Does this mean that we should only allow our children to marry people who are just like us? Or that we should return to the idea of primogeniture, where the firstborn gets everything? Obviously not. But it certainly means that we need to keep our family values strong and encourage our children to marry people who share those same values. We need to figure out ways to keep our families together, even after we are gone.

> We need to figure out ways to keep our families together, even after we are gone.

A second lesson from this story is the role of the mother in a family. Sometimes mother really does know best! We men today need to listen to the women in our lives—our wives, our mothers and grandmothers, our sisters, our daughters—as much as we listen to the other males in our lives. (This is *especially* true for those of us who are not married and are involved in an institution like the male-dominated Catholic Church.) If we don't listen to women and treat them as equals, they will have no other option except to connive and manipulate us the way Rebecca did Isaac.

Finally, another lesson from this story is that lying, cheating, and stealing have lots of consequences, and eventually there must be forgiveness and reconciliation. The rest of the story of Esau and Jacob makes that point.

Jacob asks for forgiveness—as we all must do

Shortly after Isaac gives his purloined blessing to Jacob, Esau comes in from his hunt with his own tasty meal for his father. In that moment Isaac realizes he has been deceived by Jacob. But according to the customs of the time, he cannot take back the birthright blessing from Jacob. Both father and son are outraged by this scheme. This part of the story is worth reading in detail.

Esau, hearing his father's words, sobbed violently and most bitterly, and cried to his father, "My father! Can't you also bless me?"

"Your brother," he said, "came here falsely and took your blessing."

Esau said, "Not for nothing was he named Jacob, the Heel. Twice now he's tricked me: first he took my birthright and now he's taken my blessing."

He begged, "Haven't you kept back any blessing for me?"

Isaac answered Esau, "I've made him your master, and all his brothers his servants, and lavished grain and wine on him. I've given it all away. What's left for you, my son?"

"But don't you have just one blessing for me, Father? Oh, bless me my father! Bless me!" Esau sobbed inconsolably.

Isaac said to him,

> *You'll live far from Earth's bounty,*
> *remote from Heaven's dew.*
> *You'll live by your sword, hand-to-mouth,*
> *and you'll serve your brother.*
> *But when you can't take it any more*
> *you'll break loose and run free.*

Esau seethed in anger against Jacob because of the blessing his father had given him; he brooded, "The time for mourning my father's death is close. And then I'll kill my brother Jacob."
Genesis 27:34-41

When Rebekah found out about Esau's murderous intent, she called Jacob aside and warned him.

"Son, listen to me. Get out of here. Run for your life to Haran, to my brother Laban. Live with him for a while until your brother cools down, until his anger subsides and he forgets what you did to him. I'll then send for you and bring you

back. Why should I lose both of you the same day?"

Rebekah spoke to Isaac, "I'm sick to death of these Hittite women. If Jacob also marries a native Hittite woman, why live?"

Genesis 27:44-46

Even Isaac agreed with this plan, not so much out of fear of Esau, but because both he and Rebekah had no use for the Canaanite women around them, and they wanted Jacob to marry a woman of their own clan. So Jacob set out for his uncle's home.

Let's pause for a moment and reflect on these events. "Sibling rivalry" has become standard vocabulary for the tensions and competitiveness that sometimes develops between brothers/sisters. Sometimes there is a basis in reality for this. One or both parents may favor one of the children, creating resentment in the other(s). Other times the feeling of envy rises from within, based on a perceived sense of inferiority: "I guess I'm just not as good as my sibling(s)." The rivalry seldom blossoms into violence, however. Usually it is more like a low simmer that occasionally bursts into flame. In any case, it has to be dealt with, especially if it persists into adult life. On their part, fathers need to be aware of their own tendency to favor one child over others. At the level of emotion, the feeling may be normal and spontaneous with no cause for guilt. But at the behavioral level, one needs to guard against subtle or overt favoritism.

Another issue in this story is the consequences of Jacob's deception. Even the Bible itself later condemns Jacob's action. The prophet Jeremiah sees the Israel of his time as imitating Jacob: "Brother schemes against brother, like old cheating Jacob" (Jeremiah 9:3-4). The truth is, Jacob (and his mother) had other options. They could have called for a family conference to talk about the birthright and who has valid claim to it. They could have proposed a compromise, perhaps a 50-50 split. But, like his grandfather, Abraham, Jacob is a good and decent man but not without his own flaws. And his sins will follow him until he asks for forgiveness.

Jacob encounters God—as we all do, one way or another

But first, let's return to Jacob's story. At this point, he is only about seventeen. One night, he lies down to sleep. We can imagine his feelings: fear, loneliness, uncertainty about his future. Suddenly, he has a wonderful dream: a stairway rising from earth to the heavens above, with angels walking up and down the stairs.

> *Then GOD was right before him, saying, "I am GOD, the God of Abraham your father and the God of Isaac. I'm giving the ground on which you are sleeping to you and to your descendants. Your descendants will be as the dust of the Earth; they'll stretch from west to east and from north to south. All the families of the Earth will bless themselves in you and your descendants."*
>
> *Genesis 28:13-14*

God reveals that he is the God of Jacob's own grandfather and father. And God renews the promises he made to them: to give Jacob and his descendants the land on which he was lying and to make them as numerous as the dust of the Earth. Then God adds this wonderful promise:

> *"I'll stay with you, I'll protect you wherever you go, and I'll bring you back to this very ground. I'll stick with you until I've done everything I promised you."*
>
> *Jacob woke up from his sleep. He said, "GOD is in this place— truly. And I didn't even know it!" He was terrified. He whispered in awe, "Incredible. Wonderful. Holy. This is God's House. This is the Gate of Heaven."*
>
> *Genesis 28:15-17*

When Jacob woke up from his dream, he felt like a new man. He had a profound sense of confidence that the God of his ancestors would accompany him, not only on this journey, but throughout his life. As we will see, "I will be with you"—words from the mouth of God—is a constant refrain through all the Scriptures. Jacob felt the need to mark this special place. He took a stone, poured oil over it, and set it up as a memorial stone. He gave a name to the place: "Bethel," meaning "house of God." Then he made a vow: he would give one-tenth of all he would possess to God (see Genesis 28:16-22).

In a time of crisis, we have some kind of spiritual experience that God is real.

We can think of this experience as Jacob's spiritual awakening. From being an insecure mama's boy and a conniver, he is beginning to have confidence—not so much in himself but in the promises of God. Many of us men recognize ourselves in this story. In a time of doubt/stress/fear/failure, we have some kind of spiritual experience that convinces us that God is real, that God is here for us, that we can trust God to guide us through the challenges of life. Some men come to this awareness fairly early in life; others do so much later, often in a time of crisis or a series of setbacks.

Jacob struggles in his marriage—just as many do

Jacob arrives safely in the land of Haran. He first encounters his uncle Laban's shepherds and reveals his identity as the son of Laban's sister Rebekah. While Jacob is talking to the shepherds, one of Laban's daughters, Rachel, arrives at the well to draw water. When Jacob sees how beautiful she is, he is smitten. Laban receives him kindly, and Jacob offers to work for him. After a month, his uncle said he should receive some kind of wage for his work: "What would he like?" Jacob proposes that he work seven years for Laban's younger daughter Rachel. Laban agreed. The Bible adds this lovely line: "So Jacob worked seven years for Rachel. But it only seemed like a few days, he loved her so much" (Genesis 29:20). Many married men can relate well to that feeling, but note that, according to the culture, sexual relations were not allowed until after the wedding. So, despite his longing for the one he loved, Jacob had to exercise sexual restraint for a long time. Even worse, he had to marry his wife's sister first!

When the seven years were up, Jacob asked to marry Rachel. Laban agreed and prepared the wedding banquet. But when it came time for the sexual consummation, Laban gave him Rachel's sister Leah instead. According to custom, the bride was veiled when she came to bed. That's why Jacob didn't realize he had the wrong girl. When he awoke in the morning and found Leah in his bed, he was enraged. He went to Laban and demanded: "What have you done to me? Didn't I work all this time for the hand of Rachel? Why did you cheat me?" (Interesting: the cheater has now been cheated!) Laban explained that it is the custom in his country that the oldest daughter must be married first. If Jacob agrees to work another seven years, he can have Rachel as well right then. Jacob agreed, and Laban finally gave him the younger daughter as his second wife. Between the two women, Jacob had twelve sons and one daughter. He became a devoted family man, as well as an effective herdsman.

In fact, Jacob was becoming so wealthy with his flocks that Laban and his family were becoming resentful. So God directed Jacob: "Go back home where you were born. I'll go with you" (Genesis 31:3). Jacob and his family leave while Laban is away. But when he returns, Laban is furious. He overtakes them and demands to know why they left. Jacob says he was afraid Laban would not let his daughters go and would demand the return of his flocks. There was also a dispute over money: "For twenty years I've done this: I slaved away fourteen years for your two daughters and another six years for your flock and you changed my wages ten times. If the God of my father, the GOD of Abraham and the Fear of Isaac, had not stuck with me, you would have sent me off penniless. But God saw the fix I was in and how hard I had worked and last night rendered his verdict" (Genesis 31:41-42). Finally, however, both men thought better of it. They agreed they had wronged each other and reconciled. Laban allows them to leave peacefully.

Jacob reconciles with his brother— as all of us must

But once again Jacob is fearful. He is returning to his own land and family, but he knows he will have to face his brother Esau, who has vowed to kill him. Perhaps Esau has had a change of heart, but Jacob cannot assume that. Jacob sends messengers ahead to Esau, assuring him that he comes in peace. When the messengers return, they tell Jacob that Esau, accompanied by 400 men, is coming to meet him. Jacob is so convinced he will be attacked by Esau that he divides his extended family and his flocks into two groups, reasoning that if one group is wiped out, the other may survive. Then he gathers gifts for Esau—sheep, camels, cows and bulls—and tells his men to offer them to Esau as a gesture of peace. While they go ahead, Jacob stays back and prays, reminding God of his earlier promises. Then ensues one of the strangest—and in some ways funniest—stories in the Scriptures:

> But during the night he got up and took his two wives, his two maidservants, and his eleven children and crossed the ford of the Jabbok. He got them safely across the brook along with all his possessions.
>
> But Jacob stayed behind by himself, and a man wrestled with him until daybreak. When the man saw that he couldn't get the best of Jacob as they wrestled, he deliberately threw Jacob's hip out of joint.
>
> The man said, "Let me go; it's daybreak."
>
> Jacob said, "I'm not letting you go 'til you bless me."
>
> The man said, "What's your name?"
>
> He answered, "Jacob."
>
> The man said, "But no longer. Your name is no longer Jacob. From now on it's Israel (God-Wrestler); you've wrestled with God and you've come through."

Jacob asked, "And what's your name?"

The man said, "Why do you want to know my name?" And then, right then and there, he blessed him.

Jacob named the place Peniel (God's Face) because, he said, "I saw God face-to-face and lived to tell the story!"

The sun came up as he left Peniel, limping because of his hip. (This is why Israelites to this day don't eat the hip muscle; because Jacob's hip was thrown out of joint.)
Genesis 32:22-32

From then on, Jacob is often referred to as "Israel" and his descendants as "Israelites." However, Jacob has suffered another wound: he walks with a limp the rest of his life. At the same time, he carries within himself the promise and the covenant between God and his people. It is a powerful story indeed. It reminds us that no matter how we may be hurt and wounded by life, the presence and blessing of God remain with us.

When morning breaks, Jacob looks up and sees Esau approaching with his 400 men. But, with the strength of God ("Israel"), Jacob limps toward Esau, bowing seven times to the ground before reaching him. To his amazement, Esau does no harm. He asks to meet all of Jacob's family, and then asks the purpose of all the gifts Jacob offered him.

Jacob says: "I was hoping that they would pave the way for my master to welcome me."

Esau says, "Oh, brother. I have plenty of everything—keep what is yours for yourself."

Jacob says, "Please. If you can find it in your heart to welcome me, accept these gifts. When I saw your face, it was as the face of God smiling on me. Accept the gifts I have brought for you. God has been good to me and I have more than enough."

Jacob urged the gifts on him and Esau accepted.
Genesis 33:8-11

So here we have an inspiring example of forgiveness and reconciliation between two brothers who had been enemies much of their lives. We especially admire Esau, the wronged brother, moved beyond his anger and hatred to a point where he was able to let go of his desire for revenge. After this incident, Jacob and his family returned to Bethel ("house of God"), the place where God first appeared to him in the dream and promised to guide him in all his ways:

> *Jacob told his family and all those who lived with him, "Throw out all the alien gods which you have, take a good bath and put on clean clothes, we're going to Bethel. I'm going to build an altar there to the God who answered me when I was in trouble and has stuck with me everywhere I've gone since."*
>
> *Genesis 35:2-3*

And there God made Jacob yet another promise:

> *I am The Strong God.*
> *Have children! Flourish!*
> *A nation—a whole company of nations!—*
> *will come from you.*
> *Kings will come from your loins;*
> *the land I gave Abraham and Isaac*
> *I now give to you,*
> *and pass it on to your descendants.*
>
> *Genesis 35:11-12*

Jacob learned his lessons—as we must

The Jacob story is a wonderful example of the male spiritual journey. The great myths and classic literature of the world are filled with similar stories. Typically, the man begins with a sense that he is called to greatness, some goal for which he must be willing to work hard and make sacrifices. But at some point he experiences failure, setback, pain, rejection—some kind of "wounding"—not once but perhaps many times. Always the temptation is there to quit, to turn back or give up—to withdraw into resentment and self-pity. But if the man can let himself be taught, formed, purified, humbled—he will be able to grow to personal and spiritual maturity. Like Jacob, he may spend the rest of his life limping, but he will be carrying within himself the promise of God to guide and direct him in his quest for wholeness and genuine character development. We will see this theme played out in the rest of the male biblical figures we will be studying.

Another key task for our journey, especially in mid-life, is to deal with unfinished business. One of these is to work at healing strained or broken relationships. Jacob was able to return home in peace because he had reconciled with both Laban and Esau.

This will often involve asking and granting forgiveness, and perhaps swallowing our pride. Note: forgiving does not mean denying there was an injury—there often was. But instead of nursing the hurt feelings, we make a decision to let them go. We may or may not need to talk to the one who hurt us; that depends on the circumstances. If we were the offender, however, we may need to make the first move: to offer an apology and ask for forgiveness.

> A key task for our journey, especially in mid-life, is to deal with unfinished business.

It may take time and prayer to reach the point of wanting to do this. But it is a request that God will always grant, because it is in accord with the divine plan for the world. The danger is that we may postpone these gestures until it is too late—that is, until someone has died. The same holds true for other healing actions, such as telling others you love them. We men often balk at this, claiming that others should know we love them because of our kindness and our actions toward them. But the fact remains: most people need to hear us speak the actual words: "I love you; I hope you know that."

One final task: We may need to forgive ourselves for whatever mistakes, sins, wrong judgments, or inappropriate actions we may have taken in our lives. Some of us have little trouble forgiving others, but cannot seem to forgive ourselves. This may stem from an unhealthy perfectionism or inability to accept our humanness. There is a marvelous passage on God's mercy from the prophet Micah that says:

> *Where is the god who can compare with you—*
> *wiping the slate clean of guilt,*
> *Turning a blind eye, a deaf ear,*
> *to the past sins of your purged and precious people?*
> *You don't nurse your anger and don't stay angry long,*
> *for mercy is your specialty. That's what you love most.*
> *And compassion is on its way to us.*
> *You'll stamp out our wrongdoing.*
> *You'll sink our sins*
> *to the bottom of the ocean.*
> *You'll stay true to your word to Father Jacob*
> *and continue the compassion you showed*
> *Grandfather Abraham—*
> *Everything you promised our ancestors*
> *from a long time ago.*

Micah 7:18-20

Once we have admitted and repented of our sins/mistakes/ misjudgments—they are gone, as if drowned in the depths of the ocean. And, as I once heard a pastor say, God puts a sign there that says, "No Fishing!" What he meant was: Don't keep going back and trying to dredge up those old pieces of the past. It was their conviction of God's mercy that helped Jacob and the other great men of the Bible to keep moving forward with their lives, and it will help us do so as well.

QUESTIONS FOR REFLECTION OR DISCUSSION

1. Jacob had his dream of the heavenly stairway at Bethel. Has any event helped you to come to spiritual awakening? Describe it.

2. How have you had to deal with people lying to or cheating you (like Jacob with Esau or Laban with Jacob)?

3. What were some of the wounds that life has dealt you? What have you learned from these? How was God trying to re-direct you?

4. If you still have unfinished business with relationships, what actions could you take this week to correct them?

5. Are there any areas of your life where you still need to forgive yourself? Do so now.

JOSEPH

A Model of Reconciliation

The story of Joseph has many lessons, because it is a story of jealousy, betrayal, adversity, faith, perseverance, generosity, and reconciliation. Plus, we all know the basic outlines from the Broadway musical, *Joseph and the Amazing Technicolor Dreamcoat*.

We left Jacob and his family back in Bethel, in the land of Canaan. There his wife Rachel became pregnant once again; she had already had Joseph. It was a very difficult pregnancy, and Rachel died shortly after giving birth to Benjamin, Jacob's twelfth son. (Jacob had six sons by his wife Leah; two by his wife Rachel; two each by his wives' servants. Sexual mores were a lot different then than they are now, guys!)

Each of the sons of Jacob, or Israel, later became heads of the twelve tribes of Israel under Moses. After burying Rachel, Jacob sought out his aged father Isaac, who died shortly thereafter. "He was buried with his family by his sons Esau and Jacob," the Bible notes (Genesis 35:29). This is another sign that the two brothers had been reconciled.

Joseph's brothers get jealous—as we all do at times

Chapter 37 of Genesis begins the story of Joseph. We read that Israel (Jacob) loved Joseph best of all because he was, along with Benjamin, a child of his old age. He gave his son an "elaborately embroidered coat" (Genesis 37:3). The Bible does not say "a coat of many colors," but it might well have been. It was a long robe or tunic with sleeves, like a garment worn by people who lived in palaces. Ordinary laborers would never wear such a robe. This aroused envy in the hearts of Jacob's other sons. "They grew to hate him—they wouldn't even speak to him" (Genesis 37:4).

To add fuel to the fire, one day Joseph told the family: "Listen to this dream I had. We were all out in the field gathering bundles of wheat. All of a sudden my bundle stood straight up and your bundles circled around it and bowed down to mine" (Genesis 37:6-7). You can imagine the reaction of the other brothers. You would think Joseph would keep his dreams to himself after this. Instead, he reported another dream: "I dreamed another dream—the sun and moon and eleven stars bowed down to me!" (Genesis 37:9). This time, even his father, Israel, scolded him for what seemed like his teenage arrogance.

Here is the first lesson we men have to learn: Quit bragging! And quit thinking that we are better than others! It almost never ends well. Of course, in this case, it turns out that Joseph's dreams came true, but his life might have been a lot easier had he kept his mouth shut. On the other hand, we know that God works in mysterious ways, including using our sins and weaknesses to further the divine plan for us.

Just as Jacob was his mother's favorite, Joseph was his father's. But that is often a mixed blessing, as we see here. Sometimes the price is to incur the envy of other siblings. We all know how difficult it is for parents not to have favorites among their children, at least at the emotional level. Some kids are perhaps naturally more attractive, more talented, even more enjoyable to be around than others. The challenge for us men is not to deny those normal feelings, but to learn to manage them. That is, not to let favoritism drive our actions and behaviors so as to arouse resentment. Kids who are favored must curb the tendency to flaunt their status in the face of the others. Some of us may remember the Smothers Brothers comedy show, where one routine was for Tom to stop all further dialogue by whining, "Mom always loved *you* best!" Unfortunately, the outcomes of such favoritism are not always funny; they can leave painful psychic scars if internalized too strongly.

Joseph's brothers got their revenge— as we sometimes try to do

Sometime later, the eleven other brothers were away pasturing their flocks. Israel instructed Joseph to go and see if all was well with them. When the brothers caught sight of him, they said to one another, "Here comes that dreamer. Let's kill him and throw him into one of these old cisterns; we can say that a vicious animal ate him up. We'll see what his dreams amount to" (Genesis 37:19-20).

But Reuben, the eldest of the brothers, had a different suggestion: Just throw Joseph into the cistern and leave him there, intending to rescue him later. Perhaps Reuben was trying to do the right thing, but rather than confront his brothers, he took the easy way out—with disastrous results. The brothers stripped Joseph of his embroidered coat and threw him into the dry cistern. Later, when they saw a caravan of camels loaded with spices and other exotic products from the East making their way to Egypt, the brothers hatched a new scheme: Sell Joseph to these traders for 20 pieces of silver. Reuben wasn't around for that discussion. When Reuben went back to the cistern and found Joseph gone, he was beside himself. Next the eleven brothers hatched a cover-up plan, soaking the long tunic in the blood of a goat and sending it by messenger to their father. Israel recognized the garment and deduced the worst, thinking his son had been killed by a wild beast. He was heart-broken.

> *Jacob tore his clothes in grief, dressed in rough burlap, and mourned his son a long, long time. His sons and daughters tried to comfort him but he refused their comfort. "I'll go to the grave mourning my son." Oh, how his father wept for him.*
>
> *Genesis 37:29-35*

The lesson for us today is obvious: Actions have real consequences, and we are not always able to fix our mistakes.

Joseph is tempted—as we often are

When Joseph arrived in Egypt, he was bought by a man named
Potiphar, the Pharaoh's chief steward. He worked hard and made
himself indispensable to his new boss.

> As it turned out, GOD was with Joseph and things went very
> well with him. He ended up living in the home of his Egyptian
> master. His master recognized that GOD was with him, saw
> that GOD was working for good in everything he did. He be-
> came very fond of Joseph and made him his personal aide. He
> put him in charge of all his personal affairs, turning everything
> over to him. From that moment on, GOD blessed the home
> of the Egyptian—all because of Joseph. The blessing of GOD
> spread over everything he owned, at home and in the fields,
> and all Potiphar had to concern himself with was eating three
> meals a day.
>
> Genesis 39:2-5

Trouble was brewing, however. "Joseph was a strikingly handsome man. As time went on, his master's wife became infatuated
with Joseph and one day said, 'Sleep with me'" (Genesis 39:6-7).
Numerous times she tried to seduce him, but Joseph would hear
none of it. He insisted he would not break the trust his master
placed in him, and he would not offend his God. One day, however, when all the other servants were gone from the house, Potiphar's wife again begged him for sex. This time, she laid hold of his
cloak; and when Joseph refused and ran out the door, she was left
holding the cloak. In a classic case of "a woman scorned," she saw
her opportunity for retaliation. She screamed for the other servants to come, then told them how Joseph had tried to seduce her.
When her husband returned, she told the same story to him. Potiphar was enraged and ordered Joseph to be imprisoned at once.

Ah, sex in the workplace! It is an issue that all men must be constantly aware of. Even if we remain as pure as Joseph, the issue is always there, including the possibility of false accusations. Like Joseph, we have to remain clear on how we are going to handle sexual temptation.

He wouldn't do it. He said to his master's wife, "Look, with me here, my master doesn't give a second thought to anything that goes on here—he's put me in charge of everything he owns. He treats me as an equal. The only thing he hasn't turned over to me is you. You're his wife, after all! How could I violate his trust and sin against God?"

She pestered him day after day after day, but he stood his ground. He refused to go to bed with her.

Genesis 39:8-10

We need to recall that in the culture of that time, when a slave attempted to seduce his master's wife, the ordinary penalty was death. Joseph's dreams had morphed into a nightmare—a fear that any day may be his last.

Joseph uses his talents to get ahead— as we should

But now the story takes an interesting twist:

But there in jail GOD was still with Joseph: He reached out in kindness to him; he put him on good terms with the head jailer. The head jailer put Joseph in charge of all the prisoners—he ended up managing the whole operation. The head jailer gave Joseph free rein, never even checked on him, because GOD was with him; whatever he did GOD made sure it worked out for the best.

Genesis 39:21-23

We are reminded how, even in times and places of stress and suffering, God remains present to us with his grace and strength.

So now, the chief jailer sees the ability and character of Joseph, and puts him in charge.

Not long after, two prominent men in the royal service—Pharaoh's chief cup-bearer and the chief baker—are brought into the prison. We are not told what their offenses were, but one day Joseph notices that both seem troubled and asks what is bothering them.

"What's wrong? Why the long faces?"

They said, "We dreamed dreams and there's no one to interpret them."

Joseph said, "Don't interpretations come from God? Tell me the dreams."

First the head cupbearer told his dream to Joseph: "In my dream there was a vine in front of me with three branches on it: It budded, blossomed, and the clusters ripened into grapes. I was holding Pharaoh's cup; I took the grapes, squeezed them into Pharaoh's cup, and gave the cup to Pharaoh."

Joseph said, "Here's the meaning. The three branches are three days. Within three days, Pharaoh will get you out of here and put you back to your old work—you'll be giving Pharaoh his cup just as you used to do when you were his cupbearer. Only remember me when things are going well with you again—tell Pharaoh about me and get me out of this place. I was kidnapped from the land of the Hebrews. And since I've been here, I've done nothing to deserve being put in this hole."

When the head baker saw how well Joseph's interpretation turned out, he spoke up: "My dream went like this: I saw three wicker baskets on my head; the top basket had assorted pastries from the bakery and birds were picking at them from the basket on my head."

Joseph said, "This is the interpretation: The three baskets are three days; within three days Pharaoh will take off your head, impale you on a post, and the birds will pick your bones clean."

And sure enough, on the third day it was Pharaoh's birthday and he threw a feast for all his servants. He set the head cupbearer and the head baker in places of honor in the presence of all the guests. Then he restored the head cupbearer to his cupbearing post; he handed Pharaoh his cup just as before. And then he impaled the head baker on a post, following Joseph's interpretations exactly.

But the head cupbearer never gave Joseph another thought; he forgot all about him.

Genesis 40:7-23

Joseph used his talent at reading dreams. Although he admitted that his talent came from God, it didn't seem to help him right away, but it time it would. That is another lesson for us men to learn: keep doing what we are good at, and eventually it will pay off. And don't forget to give God some of the credit.

Joseph comes out on top—as we sometimes do

Two years passed. Now it was Pharaoh's turn to have dreams. He was standing at the Nile River, when suddenly seven cows came up out of the water. They looked healthy and fat, and were grazing in the reed grass. Behind them were seven other cows, thin and ugly, and they proceeded to devour the fat cows. Pharaoh woke up in a sweat. Falling asleep again, he had another dream. He saw seven ears of grain, fat and healthy, but behind them were seven other ears, thin and sick-looking. They swallowed up the healthy ears of grain.

In the morning Pharaoh was deeply agitated. He summoned all the magicians and sages of Egypt, but none of them could interpret his dreams. Then the cupbearer had a sudden retrieval of memory. He told Pharaoh how he and the baker had strange dreams, and how the Hebrew prisoner Joseph had so brilliantly interpreted them. The Pharaoh sent for Joseph and asked him to interpret his two dreams. Joseph answered, "Not I, but God. God will set Pharaoh's mind at ease" (Genesis 41:16).

Then he proceeded to explain the dreams. "They are telling you," said Joseph, "that Egypt is going to enjoy seven years of good weather and abundant crops, followed by seven years of drought and severe famine. And this is going to happen very soon. Here's what you must do: Find a wise and trustworthy man, put him in charge of the land of Egypt, and give him some assistants who will oversee the storage of grain during the abundant years."

Joseph had interpreted his way into a great job:

> Then Pharaoh said to his officials, "Isn't this the man we need? Are we going to find anyone else who has God's spirit in him like this?"
>
> So Pharaoh said to Joseph, "You're the man for us. God has given you the inside story—no one is as qualified as you in experience and wisdom. From now on, you're in charge of my affairs; all my people will report to you. Only as king will I be over you."
>
> So Pharaoh commissioned Joseph: "I'm putting you in charge of the entire country of Egypt." Then Pharaoh removed his signet ring from his finger and slipped it on Joseph's hand. He outfitted him in robes of the best linen and put a gold chain around his neck. He put the second-in-command chariot at his disposal, and as he rode people shouted "Bravo!"
>
> Joseph was in charge of the entire country of Egypt.
> *Genesis 41:38-43*

The story of Joseph's rise to power is an example of how we can overcome envy, injustice, and even violence in our lives and still come out on top. Notice how God never abandoned Joseph in Egypt. By sticking to his faith, values, and trustworthiness, he gained the respect of the chief steward Potiphar, his jailer, and the pharaoh. Events that seem harsh and even tragic often help us rely more deeply on God's grace and wisdom. Even when Joseph was falsely accused of attempted adultery and imprisoned for it, he did not waste energy in self-pity. For example, he was helpful to the chief jailer in managing the prison and genuinely cared for the other prisoners, and when he noticed the troubled mood of the cupbearer and the baker, he offered to help them. Those traits were finally noticed and rewarded, as they will be in our own lives if, like Joseph, we stick to our spiritual principles and practices.

We admire men who can rise above the needs of their own ego and extend themselves in generous service.

Again, we have all met people who have the spiritual capacity to rise above their painful circumstances and maintain a positive attitude toward their suffering. Stories from the Nazi concentration camps and the Soviet gulags tell of prisoners who gave away their own crust of bread to one who was more needy or to a priest to be able to offer Mass for the prisoners in the dead of night.

Finally, we are inspired by the ability of Joseph to overlook his own unjust treatment and offer leadership in averting a disastrous famine in the country in which he was an alien and an innocent victim of trumped-up charges. He could have simply interpreted Pharaoh's dreams and then walked away, saying "Bad times are ahead, folks. You'd better get ready!" Instead, he laid out a realistic plan for averting the upcoming famine. Moreover, he agreed to administer the operation, taking responsibility for building the storage bins, collecting the surplus grain, and later overseeing the distribution during the years of crop failure. Joseph proved himself much more than a dreamer and interpreter of dreams. He also showed practical ability for creative planning, leadership, and organizational skills. We admire men like this who can rise above the needs of their own ego and extend themselves in generous service to their country, their community, and their church. They are truly men of character.

Joseph bails out his family— as we often have to do

Meanwhile, back in the land of Canaan, Jacob (Israel) and his family were suffering from the effects of the famine there. He told his sons to stop gawking at each other and do something. We've heard there is plenty of grain in Egypt; go down there and buy some for us So ten of the brothers set out for Egypt; their father insisted that young Benjamin not go along, lest something harmful should happen to him as it had to his full brother, Joseph.

When the brothers came into Joseph's presence, they knelt down before him with their faces to the ground. They did not recognize him, of course. He was one of the most powerful men in the world and, besides, they had assumed long ago that he was probably dead. However, Joseph recognized them but spoke to them through an interpreter. He was harsh to them at first, accusing them of being spies, but they insisted they were simply sons of an elderly man in Canaan coming to purchase food for the family, including the youngest brother at home. Joseph desperately wanted to see his full brother Benjamin, who was very young when Joseph had been sold into slavery. So, he told the brothers he would have to test them in one of the most touching exchanges in the Bible:

Joseph spoke to them. "Do this and you'll live. I'm a God-fearing man. If you're as honest as you say you are, one of your brothers will stay here in jail while the rest of you take the food back to your hungry families. But you have to bring your youngest brother back to me, confirming the truth of your speech—and not one of you will die." They agreed.

Then they started talking among themselves. "Now we're paying for what we did to our brother—we saw how terrified he was when he was begging us for mercy. We wouldn't listen to him and now we're the ones in trouble."

Reuben broke in. "Didn't I tell you, 'Don't hurt the boy'? But no, you wouldn't listen. And now we're paying for his murder."

Joseph had been using an interpreter, so they didn't know that Joseph was understanding every word. Joseph turned away from them and cried. When he was able to speak again, he took Simeon and had him tied up, making a prisoner of him while they all watched.

Genesis 42:21-24

The brothers agreed; but when they left Joseph's presence they agonized with each other for having sold Joseph into slavery, especially when they discovered that the money they had left with the steward as payment for the supplies he had given them showed up in their sacks. When they returned to their father and told them everything that had happened, Jacob was appalled at the thought of letting his youngest son go, saying "My son will not go down with you. His brother is dead and he is all I have left. If something bad happens to him on the road, you'll put my gray, sorrowing head in the grave" (Genesis 42:38).

But when the food they had brought began to run short, Jacob finally relented and told his sons to go back to Egypt for more. But his son Judah reminded him that they dare not appear without their youngest brother:

Let the boy go; I'll take charge of him. Let us go and be on our way—if we don't get going, we're all going to starve to death— we and you and our children, too! I'll take full responsibility for his safety; it's my life on the line for his. If I don't bring him back safe and sound, I'm the guilty one; I'll take all the blame. If we had gone ahead in the first place instead of procrastinating like this, we could have been there and back twice over.

Genesis 43:8-10

Jacob sent his sons off with great trepidation: "If it has to be, it has to be. But do this: stuff your packs with the finest products from the land you can find and take them to the man as gifts— some balm and honey, some spices and perfumes, some pistachios and almonds. And take plenty of money—pay back double what was returned to your sacks; that might have been a mistake. Take your brother and get going. Go back to the man. And may The Strong God give you grace in that man's eyes so that he'll send back your other brother along with Benjamin. For me, nothing's left; I've lost everything" (Genesis 43:14).

We see here the real anguish on the parts of both the brothers and their father. They finally accepted responsibility for all they had done, not knowing how it would turn out. They only did this, however, because they were desperate. Isn't that how we often act as well? Wouldn't it be better if we could admit up front what we had done, express our sorrow for it, resolve never to do it again, and then try to make up for it? That is, as you know, the Catholic formula for reconciliation. We have a whole sacrament to deal with sin!

I have noted both the greatness of character as well as the flaws in Abraham and in Jacob. The theme continues in the figure of Joseph. We cannot but admire his ability to rise above his circumstances: being sold into slavery in a foreign land; wrongfully imprisoned on a trumped-up charge of adultery; helping a fellow prisoner and then being forgotten by him. Still, he is willing to help his captors to avoid severe famine by directing them toward wise planning.

We are put off by the way Joseph toys with his brothers when they come to buy food. He pretends not to know them and accuses them (the falsely accused now becomes the unjust accuser!) of being spies. He throws them all into prison, then decides to hold only one of them—on condition they bring their youngest brother to him. He must have known this would be a terrible trial for his father. Why did he do these things? The Bible doesn't give us clear motives. Most likely it was simple payback for the brothers' past cruelty to him.

Anyway, the brothers took off with young Benjamin in their company. They dealt with Joseph's steward about the money that had been put back in their bags on their previous trip, and he assured them that he had been paid in full. They then presented their gifts to Joseph when he came in to see them. There ensued this touching reunion:

> Joseph welcomed them and said, "And your old father whom you mentioned to me, how is he? Is he still alive?"
>
> They said, "Yes—your servant our father is quite well, very much alive." And they again bowed respectfully before him.
>
> Then Joseph picked out his brother Benjamin, his own mother's son. He asked, "And is this your youngest brother that you told me about?" Then he said, "God be gracious to you, my son."
>
> Deeply moved on seeing his brother and about to burst into tears, Joseph hurried out into another room and had a good cry. Then he washed his face, got a grip on himself, and said, "Let's eat."
>
> Joseph was served at his private table, the brothers off by themselves and the Egyptians off by themselves (Egyptians won't eat at the same table with Hebrews; it's repulsive to them). The brothers were seated facing Joseph, arranged in order of their age, from the oldest to the youngest. They looked at one another wide-eyed, wondering what would happen next. When the brothers' plates were served from Joseph's table, Benjamin's plate came piled high, far more so than his brothers. And so the brothers feasted with Joseph, drinking freely.
>
> Genesis 43:27-34

Then the story takes a disturbing twist. Joseph orders his steward to fill the brothers' sacks with grain for their return journey. He also tells him to place his own silver drinking goblet into the top of Benjamin's sack. After the brothers left, he ordered the steward to catch up with them and accuse them of stealing the goblet. The brothers protest their innocence and invite the steward to search their sacks, swearing that if it is found, the one who has it will die and the others will become Joseph's slaves. To their horror, the goblet is found in Benjamin's sack.

They had to return to Joseph's palace. There they flung themselves on the ground while Joseph demanded to know how they could have done such an ungrateful deed. The brothers confessed, even though that hadn't done anything, and offered to become Joseph's slaves for life. Joseph insisted that only the thief, young Benjamin, should become a slave. The rest of them could go home. But Judah gave a heart-rending speech to Joseph, telling him about his aging father and how Jacob had already lost one son: "So let me stay here as your slave, not this boy. Let the boy go back with his brothers. How can I go back to my father if the boy is not with me? Oh, don't make me go back and watch my father die in grief!" (Genesis 44:33-34).

At that point, Joseph could no longer contain himself. He ordered all his servants to leave the room and turned to his brothers.

"I am Joseph your brother whom you sold into Egypt. But don't feel badly, don't blame yourselves for selling me. God was behind it. God sent me here ahead of you to save lives. There has been a famine in the land now for two years; the famine will continue for five more years—neither plowing nor harvesting. God sent me on ahead to pave the way and make sure there was a remnant in the land, to save your lives in an amazing act of deliverance. So you see, it wasn't you who sent me here but God. He set me in place as a father to Pharaoh, put me in charge of his personal affairs, and made me ruler of all Egypt.

"Hurry back to my father. Tell him, 'Your son Joseph says: I'm master of all of Egypt. Come as fast as you can and join me here. I'll give you a place to live in Goshen where you'll be close to me—you, your children, your grandchildren, your flocks, your herds, and anything else you can think of. I'll take care of you there completely. There are still five more years of famine ahead; I'll make sure all your needs are taken care of, you and everyone connected with you—you won't want for a thing.'

"Look at me. You can see for yourselves, and my brother Ben-jamin can see for himself, that it's me, my own mouth, telling you all this. Tell my father all about the high position I hold in Egypt, tell him everything you've seen here, but don't take all day—hurry up and get my father down here."

Then Joseph threw himself on his brother Benjamin's neck and wept, and Benjamin wept on his neck. He then kissed all his brothers and wept over them. Only then were his brothers able to talk with him.

Genesis 45:5-15

When the brothers returned to their father, Jacob, and told him Joseph was alive and held a high office in Egypt, he was dumbfounded. But when he saw the wagons Joseph had provided for his move to Egypt, his spirits revived: "I've heard enough—my son Joseph is still alive. I've got to go and see him before I die" (Genesis 45:28). With that, the caravan of Jacob and his ex-tended family, together with all their livestock and possessions, migrated to Egypt. Sometime later, Jacob died peacefully there, after instructing his sons to bury him back in the land of Canaan, beside the graves of Abraham and Sarah, Isaac and Rebekah, and his own wives Rachel and Leah.

Joseph is finally reconciled—as we all must be

But there was one last piece of unfinished business.

After burying his father, Joseph went back to Egypt. All his brothers who had come with him to bury his father returned with him. After the funeral, Joseph's brothers talked among themselves: "What if Joseph is carrying a grudge and decides to pay us back for all the wrong we did him?"

So they sent Joseph a message, "Before his death, your father gave this command: Tell Joseph, 'Forgive your brothers' sin—all that wrongdoing. They did treat you very badly.' Will you do it? Will you forgive the sins of the servants of your father's God?"

When Joseph received their message, he wept.

Then the brothers went in person to him, threw themselves on the ground before him and said, "We'll be your slaves."

Joseph replied, "Don't be afraid. Do I act for God? Don't you see, you planned evil against me but God used those same plans for my good, as you see all around you right now—life for many people. Easy now, you have nothing to fear; I'll take care of you and your children." He reassured them, speaking with them heart-to-heart.

Joseph continued to live in Egypt with his father's family. Joseph lived 110 years. He lived to see Ephraim's sons into the third generation. The sons of Makir, Manasseh's son, were also recognized as Joseph's.

At the end, Joseph said to his brothers, "I am ready to die. God will most certainly pay you a visit and take you out of this land and back to the land he so solemnly promised to Abraham, Isaac, and Jacob."

Then Joseph made the sons of Israel promise under oath, "When God makes his visitation, make sure you take my bones with you as you leave here."

Genesis 50:14-25

We must not overlook the spiritual growth taking place in the other brothers. They are no longer blaming one another for what they all conspired to do to Joseph; they took collective responsibility for their action. They also showed deep compassion for their elderly father. However, it was Judah especially who stands out as the mature man in this story. It is not surprising that the Bible traces the lineage of Jesus through the family of David, to the tribe of Judah.

Finally, we see the noble side of Joseph emerge profoundly in his willingness to completely forgive his brothers and to be reconciled with them. And he clearly attributes to the providence of God all that has happened to him: "God was behind it" (Genesis 45:6).

One of the marks of spiritual maturity is the ability to look back at our lives and see the guidance and blessings of God, even when we were passing through stressful, difficult times.

This is the ending of the book of Genesis. The descendants of Abraham/Sarah, Isaac/Rebekah, Jacob/Rachel and Jacob/Leah are now dwelling as immigrants in the land of Egypt. For the moment they are treated well by the Egyptians because of their respect for the Hebrew Joseph. But trouble is brewing on the horizon....

QUESTIONS FOR REFLECTION AND DISCUSSION

1. Have you ever been falsely accused of some wrong action or omission? How did you deal with it? What did you learn from it?

2. The Pharaoh's cup-bearer promised to put in a good word for Joseph in prison, but he "forgot" to do it. How have you had to deal with broken promises?

3. Joseph got his break from prison when Pharaoh's courtiers were unable to interpret his dreams. Have there been times in your life when you were helped in a surprising, unpredictable way? How did that affect you spiritually?

4. When have been called upon (or volunteered) to help solve a problem in the family, in the workplace, or in the civic or church community? What obstacles did you have to face and how did you overcome them?

5. Does the Joseph story connect with your own life? Describe how.

MOSES

Portrait of a Spiritual-Political Leader

There's not a lot of good political leadership around today. In fact, there's even less *spiritual-political* leadership. Here is the story of one man who was able to combine both, and, in the process, set salvation history in motion.

The book of Genesis ends with the death of Joseph. The next book, Exodus, reminds us that all of his extended family had migrated to Egypt and notes that "the children of Israel kept on reproducing. They were very prolific—a population explosion in their own right—and the land was filled with them" (Exodus 1:6-7).

The next verse is an ominous one:

A new king came to power in Egypt who didn't know Joseph. He spoke to his people in alarm, "There are way too many of these Israelites for us to handle. We've got to do something: Let's devise a plan to contain them, lest if there's a war they should join our enemies, or just walk off and leave us."

So they organized them into work-gangs and put them to hard labor under gang-foremen. They built the storage cities Pithom and Rameses for Pharaoh. But the harder the Egyptians worked them the more children the Israelites had—children everywhere! The Egyptians got so they couldn't stand the Israelites and treated them worse than ever, crushing them with slave labor. They made them miserable with hard labor—making bricks and mortar and back-breaking work in the fields. They piled on the work, crushing them under the cruel workload.

Exodus 1: 8-14

The Pharaoh was growing so desperate now that he ordered his people to practice what we would call today gender genocide: "Every boy that is born, drown him in the Nile. But let the girls live" (Genesis 1:22).

But one day, the story goes, a Hebrew woman gave birth to a male child. She could not bear the thought of having his life extinguished. First she tried to hide him in her home. After a few months, when she realized his cries could easily attract the attention of the authorities, she placed him in a basket and hid him among the reeds of the river. One day, when Pharaoh's daughter went to bathe in the river, she spotted the basket and found the baby inside. She knew it was a Hebrew child, but she was so taken with him that she decided to adopt him as her own.

However, Moses's sister, Miriam, who was watching from the reeds along the river, approached the Pharaoh's daughter, which in itself was a courageous act:

> "Do you want me to go and get a nursing mother from the Hebrews so she can nurse the baby for you?"
>
> Pharaoh's daughter said, "Yes. Go." The girl went and called the child's mother.
>
> Pharaoh's daughter told her, "Take this baby and nurse him for me. I'll pay you." The woman took the child and nursed him.
>
> After the child was weaned, she presented him to Pharaoh's daughter, who adopted him as her son. She named him Moses (Pulled-Out), saying, "I pulled him out of the water."
>
> Exodus 2:7-10

Moses is forced to flee—as we sometimes are

Moses grew up in the palace of the Pharaoh, king of Egypt. This is not an insignificant part of the story, because it allowed him to receive a real education and understand the inner workings of the Pharaoh's court—both important things for the man who was to lead a whole group of people out of slavery and form them into a new nation.

One day, after growing into young manhood, Moses ventured away from home and saw an Egyptian slave-driver striking one of the Hebrew workers. The Bible seems to imply that Moses knew he was a Hebrew himself; at any rate, he was enraged at what he saw and killed the slave-driver. The next day, he went out again and saw two Hebrews fighting among themselves. When he tried to stop them by reminding them they were kinsmen, they replied that he was not their ruler. When they said they knew he had killed an Egyptian the day before, Moses was fearful: What if Pharaoh heard about this? So he packed up and left the palace, fleeing eastward to the land of Midian. The next scene reveals a noble side of Moses' character. While he was resting at a well, seven young women came to draw water for their father's flock. Some shepherds came and tried to drive the women away, but Moses intervened and helped the girls water their flocks. When they returned and told their father, Jethro, he told them to go back and invite Moses to their home. He gave Moses a job tending the flocks and later gave him one of his daughters, Zipporah, in marriage. They had a son, and Moses named him Gershom (Sojourner) because, he said, "I'm a sojourner in a foreign country" (Exodus 2:22).

Let's pause a moment to reflect on the Moses story so far. In our study of Jacob, we noted that the male spiritual journey usually involves some kind of wounding—failure, setback, loss, betrayal. Depending on his response, the man may either become bitter and cynical or more humble and compassionate. Another way of viewing this process is to use the language of *descent*. Joseph Campbell makes use of this theme when writing about "the hero's journey." In ancient myths, folklore, and classic literature, the male always has to undergo some kind of downward movement of pain or humiliation in order to purify himself of egoism and to open his heart to understanding the pain and suffering of other people.

So, here we have Moses' first experience of descent. All

through his childhood and adolescence, he probably had grown up pampered in the Pharaoh's palace, enjoying every kind of comfort: rich food and wine, soft bed, servants to wait on him, beautiful girls to flatter him. Then one day, his eyes are opened as he sees the pain and suffering of his own people. This is what we Catholics call the instinct for social justice. When he tries to help (with violence), however, his act is discovered and he is forced to flee as a refugee. And where does he go? To the land of Midian, a rather harsh desert land where the inhabitants have to eke out a living day-by-day. And for the first time in his life, Moses has to go to work—and for a lowly shepherd. Big time descent. In his own words: "I am a sojourner in a foreign country."

Will we allow our descents to help us grow spiritually?

I suspect every one of us men can identify with the movement of descent. Who among us has not experienced making a bad play that led to loss of the game, forgetting our lines in the school play, being rejected by the college of our choice, being dumped by a girlfriend, losing a job, being blamed for a business loss, seeing our child get into trouble and not being able to help, going through a painful divorce, developing an illness or disability, losing a loved one in death?

Because of our humanity, we simply cannot avoid the descents of life. Sometimes they are thrust upon us by others or by sheer bad luck; other times (and these are the hardest), we fall into descent through our own unwise choices or poor planning. So, the only important question is: Will we let ourselves to be defeated by descent, become bitter and cynical? Or will we allow our descents to deepen us, help us grow spiritually, and find God waiting for us in that hard place?

Moses chose the second path. Through his first descent, his character was re-formed and re-shaped. He is now ready to meet God, and his life will be forever changed. Just as ours could be.

Moses encounters a burning bush— as we may in our lives

The second chapter of Exodus ends with a poignant summary of the descent of the Hebrew people in Egypt:

> *Many years later the king of Egypt died. The Israelites groaned under their slavery and cried out. Their cries for relief from their hard labor ascended to God:*
>> *God listened to their groanings.*
>> *God remembered his covenant with Abraham, with Isaac, and with Jacob.*
>> *God saw what was going on with Israel.*
>> *God understood.*

> *Exodus 2:23-25*

God has not forgotten his people and the covenant he made with their fathers. He needed to raise up a spiritual-political leader to bring them out of slavery and make a nation out of them. He chose Moses.

One day, Moses is out tending the flock of his father-in-law (just like every other day). In leading the sheep and goats through the desert, he comes to a mountain named Horeb. Suddenly, he sees a bush on fire; but the flames are not consuming the bush. Coming closer, Moses hears the voice of God calling him by name and telling him to remove his sandals because he is standing on holy ground. (It is important to remember at this point in the story that there is no indication that Moses knows God or has any real knowledge of him. Moses was much like Abraham in this regard.)

God tells Moses he is the God of his ancestors Abraham, Isaac, and Jacob; he has seen the afflictions of the Hebrew people in Egypt and he knows what they are suffering; and he intends to deliver them and lead them into a new and fertile land. And—by the way—he wants Moses to lead this rescue mission!

Moses reacts in much the same way most of us would: "Who,

me?" Moses objects. "Who am I to go to Pharaoh and tell him to free my people? Why would the Hebrews ever listen to me? Besides, I have a speech impediment, and I'm not a good public speaker." And on and on. You know, like we would!

Does God then give Moses a five-point strategic plan for pulling off this coup? No. God simply says, "I'll be with you, And this will be the proof that I am the one who sent you: When you have brought my people out of Egypt, you will worship God right here at this very mountain"(Genesis 3:12). (These are, by the way, similar words to those God used to reassure Jacob when he had his dream of the stairway to heaven.)

Then Moses voices another worry.

"Suppose I go to the People of Israel and I tell them, 'The God of your fathers sent me to you;' and they ask me, 'What is his name?' What do I tell them?"

God said to Moses, "I-AM-WHO-I-AM. Tell the People of Israel, 'I-AM sent me to you.'"

God continued with Moses: "This is what you're to say to the Israelites: 'GOD, the God of your fathers, the God of Abraham, the God of Isaac, and the God of Jacob sent me to you.' This has always been my name, and this is how I always will be known."

Exodus 3:13-15

God goes on to tell Moses to go to the elders of Israel and tell them: "The God of your ancestors is concerned about you and the way you are being mistreated in Egypt; he has decided to lead you out of your misery and bring you to a wonderful new land." But Moses raises one more objection: "Master, please, I don't talk well. I've never been good with words, neither before nor after you spoke to me. I stutter and stammer" (Exodus 4:10). Don't Moses' excuses sound like us when are asked to do something we know needs to be done, but will be a tough challenge for us? At this point God gets irritated with Moses and scolds him for his resistance.

Finally, God gives in just a little and tells Moses that his brother, Aaron, can act as his spokesman. God says Aaron is already on his way to meet Moses as they were speaking and adds, "I'll be right there with you as you speak and with him as he speaks, teaching you step by step. He will speak to the people for you. He'll act as your mouth, but you'll decide what comes out of it" (Exodus 4:15-16).

With that, Moses left Midian and went back to Egypt. That is how Abraham, Jacob, and Joseph responded to God's call as well: They just did it. That is exactly how we need to respond.

Moses and Aaron accept their calling— as we all need to

"GOD spoke to Aaron, Go and meet Moses in the wilderness" (Exodus 4:27). He went and met Moses at the mountain of God and kissed him. Moses told Aaron the message that God had sent him to speak and the wonders he had commanded him to do.

First, the two brothers went to their own people in Egypt and shared with them what the Lord had said to Moses. Probably to their surprise, "the people trusted and listened believingly that GOD was concerned with what was going on with the Israelites and knew all about their affliction. They bowed low and they worshiped" (Exodus 4:31).

The positive attitude was short-lived, however. For when the two brothers went to ask Pharaoh to simply let the Israelites go into the desert for three days to offer sacrifice to Yahweh, the king refused in no uncertain terms.

> Pharaoh said, "And who is GOD that I should listen to him and send Israel off? I know nothing of this so-called 'GOD' and I'm certainly not going to send Israel off."
>
> They said, "The God of the Hebrews has met with us. Let us take a three-day journey into the wilderness so we can worship our GOD lest he strike us with either disease or death."

But the king of Egypt said, "Why on earth, Moses and Aaron, would you suggest the people be given a holiday? Back to work!" Pharaoh went on, "Look, I've got all these people bumming around, and now you want to reward them with time off?"

Exodus 5:2-5

The request backfired and things got much worse for the Hebrews. They turned on Moses and Aaron, saying, "May GOD see what you've done and judge you—you've made us stink before Pharaoh and his servants! You've put a weapon in his hand that's going to kill us!" (Exodus 5:21).

Of course, Moses complained to God: "My Master, why are you treating this people so badly? And why did you ever send me? From the moment I came to Pharaoh to speak in your name, things have only gotten worse for this people. And rescue? Does this look like rescue to you?" (Exodus 5:22-23).

Again, doesn't this sound like us in our times of stress? Don't we, too, lose faith when things don't go our way? We doubt ourselves. We doubt God. We doubt the strategies we have chosen. Don't we sometimes feel that we have made things worse, rather than better?

Moses undergoes many trials—as we all

Many Biblical scholars understand the plagues as natural events associated with the annual overflowing of the Nile River. Their supernatural quality (phenomena directed by God) lies in their timing. For example, the first plague happens when Aaron stretches out his staff over the Nile, and the waters turn into blood. In fact, before the Nile overflows each year, it sweeps through a mountainous region where it picks up deposits of red soil, changing the color of the water and making it unfit for drinking. The flooding could also account for the next plagues: frogs, gnats (mosquitoes), and swarms of flies. The sixth plague (boils) could be the "Nile-scab," an irritating skin eruption that occurs during the Nile flooding. The next one (hail-storms) is rare in Egypt, but it does happen occasionally during these months. The plague of locusts is quite a common occurrence in this part of the world. The ninth plague (three days of darkness) could be the well-known *khamsin*, a hot wind that blows off the desert in spring and causes darkness and a very oppressive atmosphere.

But recall this: the biblical authors, as well as the Hebrew people, clearly would have seen these phenomena as caused by God (or at least under God's direction). They would have been sure that these natural events were sent by God to convince the Pharaoh to let the slaves go free. Like any good community organizer today, Moses was using whatever he had available to make his point. More liberal scholars today tend to view the plagues as mythical ways of depicting the enormous difficulties and length of time it must have taken before the Hebrew people finally broke free of their oppression. In any case, after each one of the plagues, Pharaoh begs Moses to end it and promises to free the people. But each time he reneges on his promise.

Finally, at the direction of God, Moses announces to Pharaoh the tenth, final, and most horrendous of the plagues: the death of the first-born child of every Egyptian family and even of the Egyptian animals. But even that threat did not move the king to let the Israelites go free. In the meantime, Moses instructed the Hebrew families to observe a special ritual meal at sundown that evening. They were to kill a lamb and sprinkle its blood on their door-posts so that the angel of death would pass over their homes and not harm their children or their animals. Then they were to be ready to leave Egypt. And so it happened: every first-born Egyptian child died, including Pharaoh's own son, while those of the Hebrews were spared. This is the story we Catholics recall every Holy Thursday evening. We are reminded that Jesus is the true first-born of God and "the lamb of sacrifice" who gave his life to save us and make us beloved sons and daughters of God.

However, there is often a nagging question in the back of our minds: Doesn't this seem like a cruel action on the part of God? After all, it was the stubbornness and cruelty of Pharaoh, not the ordinary Egyptians, that kept blocking God's desire to free the Hebrew people. It may even be that the rank and file Egyptians were totally supportive of the king's desire to keep the Hebrews as slave laborers. In other words, they were complicit in his sin. Still, the punishment seems severe.

The people cross to freedom—as we will

We read that during the night Pharaoh summoned Moses and Aaron and told them to leave:

> *Pharaoh called in Moses and Aaron that very night and said, "Get out of here and be done with you—you and your Israelites! Go worship God on your own terms. And yes, take your sheep and cattle as you've insisted, but go. And bless me."*
>
> *The Egyptians couldn't wait to get rid of them; they pushed them to hurry up, saying, "We're all as good as dead."*
>
> Exodus 12:31-33

Exodus says the number of true Israelites was 600,000 men, not counting children, plus "a crowd of riffraff tagging along, not to mention the large flocks and herds of livestock" (Genesis 12:38). Most scholars say this is clearly an exaggeration (an example of Biblical hyperbole); a more realistic number might be 5,000 to 6,000. Note that a crowd of "riffraff" accompanied them. These may have been slaves who were taken into freedom by the Israelites but not descended from Jacob.

We are told they were led by God not by the most direct route (they would have to fight the Philistines), but by way of "the Red Sea" (Exodus 13:18). This is definitely not the Red Sea between present-day Egypt and Saudi Arabia. Rather, it is the Reed Sea—a shallow, marshy body of water near Bitter Lakes.

Meanwhile, back in Egypt, Pharaoh and his people are berating themselves for letting their slaves escape. So, the king ordered his soldiers and chariots and went in pursuit of the Hebrews, who were encamped at the Reed Sea. When they saw the Egyptians coming at them, they were totally afraid and cried out in terror to God.

> They told Moses, "Weren't the cemeteries large enough in Egypt so that you had to take us out here in the wilderness to die? What have you done to us, taking us out of Egypt? Back in Egypt didn't we tell you this would happen? Didn't we tell you, 'Leave us alone here in Egypt—we're better off as slaves in Egypt than as corpses in the wilderness.'"

> Moses spoke to the people: "Don't be afraid. Stand firm and watch GOD do his work of salvation for you today. Take a good look at the Egyptians today for you're never going to see them again.

> GOD will fight the battle for you.
> And you? You keep your mouths shut!"

> Exodus 14:11-14

What ensued was the story we all know. The Reed Sea dried up temporarily. (The same thing happened centuries later when the Roman general Scipio crossed over the same lagoon to capture New Carthage.) Once again God made use of natural phenomenon to further his purposes. The miraculous element was the perfect timing for the Hebrews. The "wall of water on their right and left" is another example of biblical hyperbole. By the time the Egyptians began to pursue the Israelites, the wind had shifted, bringing rain and high water back into the lagoon, clogging the chariot wheels, and drowning the soldiers.

Each year at the Easter Vigil, we Catholics listen to the story of this marvelous deliverance of God's people. We even sing the hymn that the Hebrews composed in memory of this event (see Genesis 15:1-18). We see it as a symbol of the waters of baptism, freeing us from the power of Satan and bringing us into the community of God's holy people.

It is not difficult to see the spiritual development taking place in Moses. We have already noted his descent—from pampered prince to hunted fugitive to lowly shepherd in the wilderness. These experiences have emptied him of any sense of entitlement or ego-boasting. He has been purified and pruned of self-glorification. Then, in his encounter with the living God in the burning bush, he begins to place himself at the service of God and his own people from whom he has been distant.

Moses is lacking in courage and self-confidence, and his trust in God is tenuous. He comes up with excuses for not returning to Egypt to confront Pharaoh and to lead the Israelites to freedom. But, as God keeps knocking down the excuses, Moses does not retreat from God. He listens, he begins to share God's compassion for his suffering people, and finally he agrees to take leadership. In turn, God empowers him to work wondrous signs (especially the plagues) that finally convince both the Hebrews and Pharaoh that God is real and desires people's trust and obedience. Moses, despite his self-doubts, is becoming an effective leader with a sense of mission.

> Good leadership involves helping others to recognize, use and develop their gifts.

As men, we are often called (and sometimes thrust) into roles of leadership. You become a father, a head of a work crew or a department, are promoted to a position of leadership in the church or in civic affairs. Some of us may possess natural leadership skills, but others may have to develop them on the fly or turn to a mentor. Becoming a leader can require a painful stretching. We may need the humility to ask for help, or to study a book on leadership like *Leadership: The Art of Empowering* by Keith Clark and Mike Panther.

We come to realize that good leadership involves helping others to recognize their own gifts and encouraging them to use and develop those gifts. Good leaders empower others to become leaders themselves, without yielding to domination or power games. Above all, we draw upon our faith. Like Moses, we believe that we are being led by God and are being called to a mission. We have a deep need to know we are making a positive difference in the lives of other people and doing God's work of creating a better world for our own and future generations. Often, we are drawn to strengthen our commitment to prayer: for wisdom and guidance, for courage to take risks, to seek to fulfill God's designs rather than our own. That is the kind of leadership we continue to see in Moses.

Moses deals with grumbling—as we do

As stressful as these events have been for Moses and the Israelites, they still have huge obstacles and problems. One of the strange quirks of human nature is that we so quickly forget our past troubles when we are faced with fresh ones. The Hebrews forgot their years of pain and slave labor in Egypt in face of the threat of starvation. They also forgot the awesome displays of God's power and compassion for them. So, Moses has to deal with a series of grumblings around food and water and other issues.

Is grumbling a sin? Not in itself, I would say. It is our natural response to misfortune, disappointment, loss, hardship, and the like. It's as if we are hard-wired for complaining. As a first response to painful experiences, it is not wrong. What is wrong, I believe, is grumbling without acting. We can waste abundant time and energy grumbling, lashing out at life's unfairness, consuming ourselves with self-pity. The task is to move beyond complaining to action. To their credit, the Israelites did take action; they brought their complaints to Moses and Aaron. But their deeper failure was to lose trust in God. They forgot how much and how powerfully God had already acted on their behalf; they failed to draw upon their previous experiences of divine help and deliverance.

At this point, the Exodus story takes an interesting twist. Moses' father-in-law, Jethro, has heard of the Israelites' departure from Egypt and brings Moses' wife and their two sons to visit him. After Moses tells him about his adventures, Jethro, who is a pagan priest, praises the God of the Hebrews and offers a sacrifice to God. The next day Jethro watches Moses in action with the Hebrew people.

The next day Moses took his place to judge the people. People were standing before him all day long, from morning to night. When Moses' father-in-law saw all that he was doing for the people, he said, "What's going on here? Why are you doing all this, and all by yourself, letting everybody line up before you from morning to night?"

Moses said to his father-in-law, "Because the people come to me with questions about God. When something comes up, they come to me. I judge between a man and his neighbor and teach them God's laws and instructions."

Moses' father-in-law said, "This is no way to go about it. You'll burn out, and the people right along with you. This is way too much for you—you can't do this alone. Now listen to me. Let me tell you how to do this so that God will be in this with you. Be there for the people before God, but let the matters of concern be presented to God. Your job is to teach them the rules and instructions, to show them how to live, what to do. And then you need to keep a sharp eye out for competent men—men who fear God, men of integrity, men who are incorruptible—and appoint them as leaders over groups organized by the thousand, by the hundred, by fifty, and by ten. They'll be responsible for the everyday work of judging among the people. They'll bring the hard cases to you, but in the routine cases they'll be the judges. They will share your load and that will make it easier for you. If you handle the work this way, you'll have the strength to carry out whatever God commands you, and the people in their settings will flourish also."

Moses listened to the counsel of his father-in-law and did everything he said. Moses picked competent men from all Israel

and set them as leaders over the people who were organized
by the thousand, by the hundred, by fifty, and by ten. They
took over the everyday work of judging among the people.
They brought the hard cases to Moses, but in the routine cases
they were the judges. Then Moses said good-bye to his father-
in-law who went home to his own country.

Exodus 18:13-27

The other spiritual connection we can make here is what someone has called "the Jethro Principle." That is, having the wisdom and the humility to acknowledge that we cannot do everything by ourselves. Like Moses, we often need help in dealing with all the demands put upon us. But sometimes, we stubbornly cling to the illusion that it all depends on us; and then we become fatigued, disappointed with ourselves, and resentful of others. We are too proud to ask for help. The other positive outcome of using the Jethro Principle is that it empowers others to discover and utilize their own gifts. We will see this in greater detail in a later story from Exodus.

Moses develops a great covenant with God— which we too must do

The next two chapters in Exodus are central to the entire Old Testament, and indeed, the whole Bible. In the third month after their departure from Egypt, the Israelites arrived at Mount Sinai and pitched camp there. Moses went up the mountain and had a special encounter with God. The Lord called to him and said: "Speak to the House of Jacob, tell the People of Israel: 'You have seen what I did to Egypt and how I carried you on eagles' wings and brought you to me. If you will listen obediently to what I say and keep my covenant, out of all peoples you'll be my special treasure. The whole Earth is mine to choose from, but you're special: a kingdom of priests, a holy nation'" (Exodus 19:4-5).

This covenant was a giant step forward in the evolution of

human morality. There was the solemn ceremony in which God's covenant was ratified by the people. Some animals were sacrificed, and then Moses took half of the blood and sprinkled it on the altar; the other half he sprinkled on the people. This was a powerful symbol: blood, the sign of life, is shared by both God and his people. They are joined as one. At the end, the people answered, "Everything GOD said, we'll do. Yes, we'll obey" (Exodus 24:7).

The next chapters are all about construction of the Ark of the Covenant and its furnishings, about the priests (chosen from the tribe of Levi), their vestments, and their sacred duties, especially offering sacrifices in the name of the people.

Meanwhile, the Israelites were getting bored and restless. When Moses went up on Mount Sinai and disappeared for a considerable time, the people went to Aaron and demanded that he make them an idol they could worship. So Aaron told them to bring him all their golden earrings and other jewelry which he then melted down and formed into the image of a golden calf. In Aaron's mind, this was not a false god; rather, it was intended as an image of God himself, symbolized by the strength of a young bull. However, both he and the people knew very well that God had forbidden them to make any image of God under any visible form. This was a flagrant act of disobedience.

God's response is swift and decisive. He tells Moses he is disappointed and angry with the people for their fickleness, and intends to destroy them and find a new people for Moses to lead. But Moses pleads with God: if you do this, the Egyptians will surely gloat. So God relented.

But then it was Moses' turn to be angry with the people. As he comes down the mountain carrying the two tablets of the Ten Commandments, he sees the golden calf and the people dancing around it and indulging in sexual actions. He smashes the two tablets and the calf, throwing it into the fire and reducing it to powder. Then he scolds Aaron: how could you do such a thing? Aaron makes a lame excuse: The people pressured me; so I took their jewelry, threw it into the fire—and lo, this calf came out! (It sounds much like kids today who tell the teacher, "The dog ate my homework!")

At this point, God makes known his disappointment with the Israelites, calling them "one hard-headed people" (Exodus 33:3), an image that will be repeated often in the Old Testament. Yet God tells Moses he and the people are to continue their journey to the Promised Land, and he will send an angel to guide them. Later we are told that a pillar of cloud would go before them during the day, and it would turn into a pillar of fire if they had to travel by night (see Exodus 40:36-38).

Another strong spiritual theme we see in Exodus is the dynamic of disobedience and forgiveness. It is not hard for us to identify with the Hebrews out there in the desert, growing restless and bored while Moses is absent. Without a visible, tangible sign of God's presence and comfort, we are tempted to seek relief in pleasure and excitement. Like many people today, the Israelites turned to food, music, and sex. Aaron, instead of challenging them to endurance and discipline, gives in to their demands.

Each of us knows how attractive the escape mode can be for us. There are numerous forms of the golden calf in today's culture: more possessions, luxury items, status-climbing, food and alcohol, sex and pornography. The truth is, we do need some enjoyable outlets in our life. The wise St. Thomas Aquinas wrote, "No one can live without some pleasure. That is why, if we are deprived of all innocent pleasures, we will eventually indulge in sinful ones."

Innocent pleasures—walking, a scenic drive, reading, listening to music, playing or watching games or sports, good conversation with friends—all are forms of gracious relaxation that enable us to preserve healthy balance in our lives. Then we are better able to practice endurance when excessive demands or sheer boredom assault us. "We know how troubles can develop passionate patience in us," St. Paul wrote, "and how that patience in turn forges the tempered steel of virtue, keeping us alert for whatever God will do next" (Romans 5:4). Sometimes endurance is the only spiritual option open to us, and it can strengthen our character.

Moses develops a personal relationship with God—which we too must do

We have seen how Moses' virtue was tested, and this led him to a deeper intimacy with God. It must have been tempting when God offered to wipe out the Hebrews and give Moses a new people to lead. But ancestral roots run deep, and Moses could not imagine either he or God rejecting their own people. He pleads his case, and God relents. Moses' heart is gradually being purified of self-centered ambition, so he is not afraid to talk honestly with God. And God responds by promising to accompany him personally on the journey: "I know you well and you are special to me. I know you by name" (Exodus 33:17). Here is a wonderful model for our own practice of prayer. We have the freedom to speak to God heart-to-heart, without hiding our honest doubts, struggles, or complaints. We can do that because God holds us in his personal, unconditional, covenant love. The only condition on our part is that we do not give up and abandon our trust in the goodness and love of God.

Now, the story takes a profound spiritual turn. The sacred author directs our attention to Moses' intimacy with God. We are told that whenever the people pitched camp, they would erect a special tent, the meeting tent, some distance from the camp. Anyone who wished to consult the Lord could enter the tent for that purpose. But when Moses would enter the tent, the pillar of cloud would stand at the tent's entrance while the Lord spoke with Moses. The author adds that God and Moses used to speak "face-to-face, as neighbors speak to one another" (Exodus 33:11). Moses said, "If your presence doesn't take the lead here, call this trip off right now. How else will it be known that you're with me in this, with me and your people? Are you traveling with us or not? How else will we know that we're special, I and your people, among all other people on this planet Earth?" (Exodus 33:15-16).

God invites Moses to return to the top of Mt. Sinai and to bring along two blank stone tablets. There God directs him to rewrite the Ten Commandments on the new tablets. The Lord then told Moses to again assemble the Israelites and teach them the commandments. God also gave special directives about observance of the Sabbath Day and about construction and adornment of the Ark of the Covenant, which was to contain the tablets of the commandments. The book of Exodus ends by noting that the Ark was kept in the meeting tent. Along with the pillar of cloud and fire, the Ark was a strong visible sign of God's presence among the people throughout their journey to the Promised Land.

As I noted above, "covenant" is a major theme in Scripture. We moderns are much more familiar with the language of "contract" rather than covenant. A contract is an agreement between two individuals or groups regarding some exchange of goods or services. In other words, I agree to do something for you in exchange for money or some service that you render to me. It is usually specific and time-limited. A covenant, on the other hand, is ongoing and all-encompassing. For Christians, the clearest example is marriage. Instead of a contract that says, "I will love and care for you as long as you remain young and healthy," marriage is a covenant that says, "I will love you and care for you all the days of my life and yours."

Likewise, God's covenant with the Israelite people (and by extension with the people of the church in the New Covenant) is timeless and unconditional: "I will be your God and you will be my people—forever." As we saw, the ritual act of Moses sprinkling the people with the lamb's blood was a powerful symbol of God and the people sharing life spiritually. God promises to be present and to care for the people, and they promise to be faithful to God and to obey his commandments.

In the New Testament, the ritual of baptism brings a Christian into a sharing of God's own life and unconditional love; in return, the person promises to live in accord with the teachings and values of Christ. The covenant is nourished and strengthened by participating in the sacraments, especially the Eucharist. When we fail to live in accord with Christ's commandments, we can find forgiveness and mercy in the sacrament of Reconciliation—just as the Israelites would often return to God after falling into sinful ways. Covenant is truly a wondrous mystery.

It is good for us to reflect on the fact that even a God-honoring man like Moses can get worn down by the daily grind of having to keep moving and working when you just want to escape from it all, especially when people around us keep complaining about our performance when we are trying to do our best. Like Moses, we slide into grumbling and discouragement. We may begin to question God's ways: "Why? Why is this happening? Why me?" Sometimes, indeed, our experience of adversity can lead us to discover some important truth about ourselves. Perhaps we have become too self-satisfied, or too self-centered, or too uncaring about the well-being of others. This can lead us to a new level of conversion; we decide to make some changes in our attitudes or our manner of living.

But often we simply cannot discover why we are having to struggle so mightily, or dealing with so many problems. There are no clear answers, just as God did not give Moses clear answers as to why his patience was being tested so severely. Like him, we may even think it would be easier to die than to keep living with all the stress. In those times, our best move is to renew our trust in God—just like Moses lying prostrate in the meeting tent and asking God to help him keep putting one foot in front of the other.

And sometimes, in hindsight, we do come to understand why God permitted misfortunes or setbacks to occur in our life. In my counseling work, I have listened to countless stories from people who had to endure pain-filled hardships in some parts of their lives. "But Father," they say, "if I had not gone through that I would never have had..." Then they share the gift, the insight, the virtue that came to them in the wake of that troubled period of their life. From my own life, I often recall the painful years of my adolescence and early adulthood, when I suffered from low self-confidence. But from that I learned a deep sense of compassion for the struggles and sufferings of other people at any stage of life. Our very saintly Capuchin, Fr. Solanus Casey, used to repeat often, "Blessed be God in all his designs!"

Moses dies—as each of us will

The time is now drawing near for Moses to die. Before he does, God directs him to take care of unfinished business. First, he has him summon Joshua to the meeting tent; there God commissions Joshua to succeed Moses as leader of the people: "Be strong. Take courage. You will lead the People of Israel into the land I promised to give them. And I'll be right there with you" (Deuteronomy 31:23).

Then, with great sadness, God tells Moses that the people will indeed enter the Promised Land, but they will become unfaithful to the covenant and rebellious against God and his commandments. He asks Moses to compose a song and teach it to the people; the song will remind them of all God has done for them. Then, when they are brought low because of their disobedience, they may recall the song and bring themselves back to the ways of God. "The Song of Moses" takes up the entire chapter 32 of the Book of Deuteronomy. It is worth reading.

Finally, God tells Moses to go up the mountain overlooking the Promised Land so he can view its beauty even though he will not be able to enter it. Then, just before he dies, Moses pronounces a solemn blessing on each of the twelve tribes of Israel. The book of Exodus concludes with this wonderful tribute to Moses:

> *No prophet has risen since in Israel like Moses, whom GOD knew face-to-face. Never since has there been anything like the signs and miracle-wonders that GOD sent him to do in Egypt, to Pharaoh, to all his servants, and to all his land— nothing to compare with that all-powerful hand of his and all the great and terrible things Moses did as every eye in Israel watched.*
>
> *Deuteronomy 34:10-11*

I once heard a Jewish rabbi say that some ancient rabbis would tell a story (not in the Bible) about the death of Moses. They say that Moses asked God to spare him from death since he had served the Lord so well. But the Lord reminded him: "You are human; you have to die." But when the day came, the rabbis say, God himself came down from heaven and held Moses in his arms. When Moses died, God received his last breath with a kiss. At that point, they say, a big tear rolled down the cheeks of God. Beautiful.

I have often told people: "Most of us are not bad people—but we do have bad memories." As we have seen, God warned the people through Moses not to forget: 1) all that God had done for them in freeing them from slavery in Egypt and guiding them through their long wanderings to the Promised Land; and 2) the covenant they made with God: to be obedient and faithful to his commandments and to worship him alone as their God. Like the Israelites, we have the same tendency to forget. We become preoccupied with earning a living, getting promotions, caring for our families, acquiring more possessions, and having more enjoyments. None of these are evil. But, they can easily preoccupy our time, energy, and devotion. Honoring God and growing in our spiritual life can get pushed off to the margins.

This is why we need constant reminders: What is most important? What is our primary purpose in life? Do we truly "love the Lord our God with our whole heart, and our neighbor as ourselves?" What can serve as reminders? Daily prayer, for one. At the beginning of each day, we look ahead to the tasks of that day and ask God to help us fulfill them with care and responsibility; we entrust our problems and anxieties to God; we ask for the wisdom we need to make the right decisions. At the end of the day, we spend some time thanking God for helping us with whatever the day has brought; and we ask forgiveness for ways we may have offended God or others.

Weekly Mass is another powerful reminder. We join with fellow Catholics in praising and thanking God for our blessings; we listen attentively to the reading of the Scriptures and the message of the homily, as well as the prayers. Our worship includes the wonderful experience of receiving the sacred body and blood of Jesus himself in Holy Communion. Another practice is to consecrate the time and energy for a new task to God before we begin, asking God to bless it and guide us to fulfill it well. Finally, we can nourish our spirits by reading from the Bible or some other spiritual work. If we are faithful to these kinds of practices, we will not easily drift into forgetfulness of God; rather, we will grow steadily in our spiritual life.

God's concern for foreigners is mirrored today in our efforts to care for the immigrants in our midst.

One other spiritual connection: We have seen that God insisted that his people, once settled in their new land, must not forget the poor or the foreign people living among them. If they are just and caring toward others, "There must be no poor people among you because GOD is going to bless you lavishly in this land that GOD, your God, is giving you as an inheritance, your very own land" (Deuteronomy 15:4). For us who live in a society of abundance, that is a serious challenge. I live in an inner city parish surrounded by people living in poverty. At Christmas time I am amazed at the generosity of the more privileged members of the parish for their donations of food, clothing, toys, etc. for those who are needy. At the same time, we partner with agencies and groups who are working to provide education and jobs for the poor. We try to join the works of charity with the works of justice. Finally, God's concern for foreigners is mirrored today in our efforts to care for the immigrants in our midst.

The story of Moses and the Hebrew people has profound lessons for us in every generation. It is the central story of the Old Testament. As the next chapters unfold, we will see how the chosen people of God struggle to remain faithful to the Sinai covenant, how often they fail, and how God remains faithful, always raising up holy people and prophets to lead and inspire them.

QUESTIONS FOR REFLECTION AND DISCUSSION

1. Have you ever felt inadequate for a task or challenge, and how did you deal with that feeling?

2. Do you feel called to do something you want to avoid? Write down what you think it is. Pray about it. Talk it over with someone. Then just do it.

3. How do you respond when you see an injustice? Are you tempted to react violently, or have you developed other ways of intervening? Describe what you do, why you do it, and what the results are.

4. Moses drew strength from his regular conversations with God in the meeting tent. Where/how do you find strength to continue your own spiritual journey?

5. In what way(s) are you called upon to exercise leadership right now? Where will you find the help you will need? How will you be reconciled if and when you fail?

DAVID

From Greatness to Failure— and Back Again

David is a striking example of one who started off well on the spiritual path, drifted far off the track—suffering greatly because of that, and then recovered to become a model of leadership and fidelity to God. It is important to remember that he was an ancestor of Jesus, whom the Bible frequently refers to as "son of David" because, in his human origins, he was descended from the family tree of David (see Matthew 1:6, for example).

We first meet David when the prophet Samuel is instructed by God to choose a new king for Israel, because the current king, Saul, has become arrogant and disobedient to God's ways. Samuel is sent by God to the town of Bethlehem (yes, the future scene of the birth of Jesus), to a man named Jesse (yes, a variation on the name *Yesuah*, or Jesus), and told Jesse to line up his seven sons, telling him one of them would chosen as the new king of Israel. When Samuel saw the oldest, the tall and handsome Eliab, he said to himself, *Surely this is the one.* But God said to Samuel: "Looks aren't everything. Don't be impressed with his looks and stature. I've already eliminated him. GOD judges persons differently than humans do. Men and women look at the face; GOD looks into the heart" (1 Samuel 16:7).

When the same thing happened with all Jesse's other sons, Samuel said to him:

"Is this it? Are there no more sons?"

"Well, yes, there's the runt. But he's out tending the sheep."

Samuel ordered Jesse, "Go get him. We're not moving from this spot until he's here."

Jesse sent for him. He was brought in, the very picture of health—bright-eyed, good-looking.

God said, "Up on your feet! Anoint him! This is the one."

Samuel took his flask of oil and anointed him, with his brothers standing around watching. The Spirit of God entered David like a rush of wind, God vitally empowering him for the rest of his life.

1 Samuel 16:11-13

David grows up—as we all do

For the time being, however, God allowed Saul to remain as the actual king. But, the Bible says, "the Spirit of God left Saul and in its place a black mood sent by God settled on him" (1 Samuel 16:14).Nowadays, we would probably say that the king suffered from spells of depression. Most of us have experienced this at one time or another in our lives.

Saul's servants told him about young David, who was skilled at playing the harp. Saul sent for him and took an instant liking to him. The Bible adds: "After that, whenever the bad depression from God tormented Saul, David got out his harp and played. That would calm Saul down, and he would feel better as the moodiness lifted" (1 Samuel 16:23). This is a good example of the healing power of music, whether it is a psalm, classical music, or rock and roll.

The next event was the famous story of Goliath. One of the long-time enemies of the Israelite people at that time were the Philistines, a rather fierce tribe that had settled along the Mediterranean coast. At one point their army encamped on a hill, and a six-and-a-half foot warrior named Goliath (not so tall by today's standards, but plenty big enough for three thousand years ago) taunted the army of Saul. Goliath proposed that, instead of having a major bloody battle, he would fight one of the Israelites hand-to-hand to the death with the army of the loser becoming slaves of the winner. When Saul and his warriors heard this, they were dismayed. Who in their army could possibly defeat this giant?

When young David heard about the challenge, he went to Saul and volunteered to take on the Philistine.

> *Saul answered David, "You can't go and fight this Philistine. You're too young and inexperienced—and he's been at this fighting business since before you were born."*
>
> *David said, "I've been a shepherd, tending sheep for my father. Whenever a lion or bear came and took a lamb from the flock, I'd go after it, knock it down, and rescue the lamb. If it turned on me, I'd grab it by the throat, wring its neck, and kill it. Lion or bear, it made no difference—I killed it. And I'll do the same to this Philistine pig who is taunting the troops of God-Alive. GOD, who delivered me from the teeth of the lion and the claws of the bear, will deliver me from this Philistine."*
>
> *Saul said, "Go. And GOD help you!"*
>
> 1 Samuel 17:33-37

Saul tried to clothe David in heavy armor and have him carry a large sword, but David found it all too cumbersome. Instead, he faced Goliath without protective armor and with only a sling-shot for a weapon. Most of us know how the story ends: David slings a sharp stone that strikes Goliath in the forehead. He is stunned and falls to the ground; David rushes over and cuts off Goliath's head with the giant's own sword. The Israelite army then attacked the demoralized Philistines and drove them out of the territory.

David was now ready to become king. He had done his apprenticeship under Saul and he had been tried by fire. Many of us men are called into leadership roles, but we have to make sure that we prepare ourselves and are mature enough to accept the challenge.

David takes over—as we are sometimes called to do

When David, Saul, and the army of Israel returned from their rout of the Philistines, they marched victoriously into the city. The women came out to meet them in the streets singing and shouting, "Saul kills by the thousand, David by the ten thousand!" (1 Samuel 18:7) This display of public adulation for David angered Saul; he grew jealous of David and feared losing the kingship to him. The very next day he fell into one of his depressed moods. When David tried to comfort him with music, Saul twice hurled a spear at him, but David was able to dodge it. Then Saul attempted to get rid of David by appointing him as a field officer in the army, hoping he would be killed in battle. But David continued to win battles, which only increased Saul's jealousy and fear.

A couple more times Saul sent assassins to kill David, but he managed to escape. He fled to neighboring Gentile lands, where he gathered a group of some 400 men who were either debtors to Saul or had turned against the king for other reasons. They became like a band of outlaws, conducting raids on various groups. One day, Saul heard that David was in a particular area and went to look for him. In fact, David and some of his men were hiding in a cave. Saul entered the cave "to relieve himself" (1 Samuel 24:2), as the Bible put it. Then this interesting scene occurred, telling us a lot about David.

> David's men whispered to him, "Can you believe it? This is the day GOD was talking about when he said, 'I'll put your enemy in your hands. You can do whatever you want with him.'" Quiet as a cat, David crept up and cut off a piece of Saul's royal robe.
>
> Immediately, he felt guilty. He said to his men, "GOD forbid that I should have done this to my master, GOD's anointed, that I should so much as raise a finger against him. He's GOD's anointed!" David held his men in check with these words and

wouldn't let them pounce on Saul. Saul got up, left the cave, and went on down the road.

Then David stood at the mouth of the cave and called to Saul, "My master! My king!" Saul looked back. David fell to his knees and bowed in reverence. He called out, "Why do you listen to those who say 'David is out to get you'? This very day with your very own eyes you have seen that just now in the cave GOD put you in my hands. My men wanted me to kill you, but I wouldn't do it. I told them that I won't lift a finger against my master—he's GOD's anointed. Oh, my father, look at this, look at this piece that I cut from your robe. I could have cut you—killed you!—but I didn't. Look at the evidence! I'm not against you. I'm no rebel. I haven't sinned against you, and yet you're hunting me down to kill me. Let's decide which of us is in the right. GOD may avenge me, but it is in his hands, not mine. An old proverb says, 'Evil deeds come from evil people.' So be assured that my hand won't touch you."

1 Samuel 24:3-13

Saul was touched. He asked David's forgiveness and even begged him not to harm his family when he became king of Israel. David promised him on oath. Later, while Saul and his army were in a fierce battle with the Philistines, Saul and his three sons, including David's friend Jonathan, were killed. When David got the news, he and his men went into mourning. He sang an elegy to their memory: "Oh, oh, Gazelles of Israel, struck down on your hills, the mighty warriors—fallen, fallen!" (2 Samuel 1:19).

After Saul's death, the Lord directed David to return to the land of Israel. He entered the city of Hebron, where the men of Judah anointed him king. However, the forces of Saul continued to fight those of David. But, as the Bible says, "The war between the house of Saul and the house of David dragged on and on. The longer it went on the stronger David became, with the house of Saul getting weaker" (2 Samuel 3:1).

Eventually all the tribes of Israel came to David in Hebron

and anointed him king. He and his army then moved to capture the city of Jerusalem, which was held by pagan Jebusites. David succeeded, and made the city his capital. Hence, even to this day, Jerusalem is known as the "City of David."

"GOD judges persons differently than humans do. Men and women look at the face; GOD looks into the heart" (1 Samuel 16:7). This was God's own explanation when Samuel was looking for a new king. How often in our own life have we made the mistake of judging by appearances? Nowadays in our culture it seems like appearance is everything. Think of the incredible number of television ads that focus on improving our physical appearance. Or our fixation on the cultivation of our image. Corporations, department stores, and universities spend millions to project the right image. The pursuit can even preoccupy our churches. The sexual abuse of children could have been stopped decades ago if the churches had been less focused on protecting their own image and more on protecting the children. And in our own individual lives, we need to be more concerned about how God sees our hearts than about how we appear in the eyes of others. Indeed, that focus ("God looks into the heart") can enable us to maintain inner peace when we are misjudged by others. Likewise, it can caution us against our tendency to judge others mainly by appearances.

The tragic figure of Saul invites us to reflect on the power of envy, one of the seven deadly sins. Saul was chosen by God to be the first king of Israel. He showed great promise at first, proving to be both a capable military leader and a wise civil ruler. But when young David, his protégé, began to emerge as a folk hero, Saul felt threatened. Were his dark moods the result of clinical depression, or rather the fruit of jealousy and the fear of being displaced? We do not know for certain. We do know that envy and jealousy can combine with anger to create moods of sadness and bitterness within us. Even when David tried to reassure Saul that he was not bent on replacing him as king, Saul could not let go of his negative moods.

We need to guard carefully against the two green-eyed monsters of envy and jealousy. There is some distinction between the two. Envy arises from seeing someone possessing an object or an ability that we are lacking; whereas jealousy makes us unwilling to share something we do possess but want to keep only for ourselves. Both can easily give rise to anger or depression. In any case, they dampen our spirits and rob us of the joy of life.

Both envy and jealousy spring from some inner insecurity: We see ourselves as lacking in some quality that someone else possesses; or we fear that someone may take away something (or someone) that we possess. The remedy for both envy and jealousy is a deeper confidence in God, who has endowed us and the people around us with certain gifts and abilities. Our task is to accept this reality without resentment, to deepen and develop the gifts we ourselves have been given, and to honor those gifts that God has given to others. We also need to remember that even those who appear to be more gifted than we are may be suffering interiorly in ways that are hidden from us, just as our weakness may be hidden from them.

> The remedy for both envy and jealousy is a deeper confidence in God.

I find inspiration in this story from the life of St. Francis of Assisi. Someone once said to him, "Brother Francis, be on your guard. Some people think you are a great saint, while others think you are a pious fraud." Francis replied, "Brother, what I am in the sight of God—that I am. No more, but also no less."

David messes up—as we all do at times

When David settled down as king in Jerusalem, he was only about 30 years old. One of his first matters of concern was to restore the centrality of the God of their ancestors in the lives of the people, who by then were known as the Israelites. It troubled him to think that the famous Ark of the Covenant, the primary visible symbol of God's presence among his people, had been left in a remote shrine after the Israelites had retaken it from the Philistines. So David ordered that the Ark be brought into Jerusalem. This was done with much festivity—a parade with singing, dancing, and rejoicing among the people. The Ark was placed in a tent, close to the royal palace that David had built for himself and his family. It remained there until David's son Solomon built the magnificent temple in Jerusalem and the Ark was given a special place in the temple.

Meanwhile, David felt badly about the Ark being left in a mere tent. So he consulted the prophet Nathan about building a special house for it. Nathan approved of the idea; but that night God spoke to Nathan and told him: "I don't need a special house. Tell my servant David":

> GOD has this message for you: GOD himself will build you a house! When your life is complete and you're buried with your ancestors, then I'll raise up your child, your own flesh and blood, to succeed you, and I'll firmly establish his rule. He will build a house to honor me, and I will guarantee his kingdom's rule permanently. I'll be a father to him, and he'll be a son to me. When he does wrong, I'll discipline him in the usual ways, the pitfalls and obstacles of this mortal life. But I'll never remove my gracious love from him, as I removed it from Saul, who preceded you and whom I most certainly did remove. Your family and your kingdom are permanently secured. I'm keeping my eye on them! And your royal throne will always be there, rock solid.

> *2 Samuel 7:11-16*

House in the Bible has the meaning of "family dynasty." The house or family of David will continue through the centuries until the coming of the Messiah. (This is why Jesus was called "the Son of David," and why the Gospel writers went to great lengths to show that Jesus was descended from David through his father Joseph.) In response to this wonderful promise, David broke into a beautiful prayer of praise and thanksgiving for all the blessings God had bestowed and would bestow upon him. It is the high point in the story of David.

King David went in, took his place before GOD, and prayed: "Who am I, my Master GOD, and what is my family, that you have brought me to this place in life? But that's nothing compared to what's coming, for you've also spoken of my family far into the future, given me a glimpse into tomorrow, my Master GOD! What can I possibly say in the face of all this? You know me, Master GOD, just as I am. You've done all this not because of who I am but because of who you are—out of your very heart!—but you've let me in on it.

This is what makes you so great, Master GOD! There is none like you, no God but you, nothing to compare with what we've heard with our own ears. And who is like your people, like Israel, a nation unique in the earth, whom God set out to redeem for himself (and became most famous for it), performing great and fearsome acts, throwing out nations and their gods left and right as you saved your people from Egypt? You established for yourself a people—your very own Israel!—your people permanently. And you, GOD, became their God.

"So now, great GOD, this word that you have spoken to me and my family, guarantee it permanently! Do exactly what you've promised! Then your reputation will flourish always as people exclaim, 'The GOD-of-the-Angel-Armies is God over Israel!' And the house of your servant David will remain sure and solid in your watchful presence. For you, GOD-of-the-Angel-Armies, Israel's God, told me plainly, 'I will build you a house.' That's how I was able to find the courage to pray this prayer to you.

"And now, Master GOD, being the God you are, speaking sure words as you do, and having just said this wonderful thing to me, please, just one more thing: Bless my family; keep your eye on them always. You've already as much as said that you

would, Master GOD! Oh, may your blessing be on my family permanently!"

2 Samuel 7: 18-29

Now, however, the story turns dark. While David's army is out fighting a border war, the king is home in his palace. One day after his afternoon nap, he takes a stroll on his roof-top and happens to notice a woman bathing in the home next door. The Bible notes that she was very beautiful. David inquires about her and learns that her name is Bathsheba, the wife of Uriah, one of David's soldiers. He sends for her; they have dinner and then have sex together. Some days later she sends a message to David that she is pregnant with his child. What to do? David says he will think of something.

The next day, he sends a message to his general, Joab, telling him to send Uriah to the palace. David asks Uriah how the war is going and then tells him to go home for the night. He assumes Uriah will sleep with Bathsheba and the pregnancy will be easily explained. But next morning David discovers Uriah had not gone home; he slept outdoors with other royal servants. When David asks him why, Uriah says it didn't seem right to sleep in a nice bed with his wife while the Ark is in a tent and his fellow soldiers are sleeping on the ground.

So David concocts another strategy. He invites Uriah to dine with him that evening; he gets him drunk with plenty of good wine, then sends him home. But again Uriah sleeps outdoors. Now David is desperate. He sends a letter to Joab and orders him to place Uriah in the front line in the next battle. Then, David tells Joab, when the fighting is fierce, pull your men back and let Uriah be killed. So now the Davidic cover-up is complete: everyone would assume that Uriah slept with his wife and that Bathsheba's child is his. And he would not be around to say otherwise. Not only that, but David will be free to marry Bathsheba.

But the best-laid plans don't always work out. "But GOD was not at all pleased with what David had done" (2 Samuel 11:27).

The Lord sent the prophet Nathan to David, who tells David an innocent-sounding story about a rich man who had huge flocks and lands, while a poor man had only one lamb which he loved and treated like his own child. One day the rich man had company, so he demanded that the poor man give up his lamb for the guest's dinner. On hearing this parable, David becomes livid, saying, "The man who did this ought to be lynched! He must repay for the lamb four times over for his crime and his stinginess!" (2 Samuel 12:6). Nathan looks David in the eye and says, "You're the man!" (2 Samuel 12:7). David then confesses humbly that he has sinned against God.

David and Bathsheba's child dies right after childbirth. David is racked with guilt. According to tradition, Psalm 51 was composed and recited by David at this point in his life. It is a prayer of profound repentance and a plea for mercy and forgiveness. It is worth reading in this context.

Now, a whole chain of evils is unleashed. First, David's son, Amnon, falls madly in love with his own half-sister, Tamar. He tries to seduce her, but when she resists, he rapes her. Tamar's brother, Absalom, also David's son, is enraged and kills Amnon. Absalom flees, but later, David allows him to return and forgives him. But then Absalom begins plotting to replace David as king. He and his followers intercept petitioners going to Jerusalem to speak to King David. Absalom and his men tell them no one in Jerusalem is willing to help them, but they will. So they gradually turn the people against David.

As Absalom gathers more people and an army, David becomes fearful and leaves Jerusalem. He goes to Mt. Olivet and weeps over Jerusalem and his own son's betrayal. (We can't help but notice the similarity between this scene and the one where Jesus weeps over the sins and coming destruction of Jerusalem.) Absalom then enters Jerusalem and has sex with all ten of David's concubines in broad daylight. The prophet Nathan had told David: what you have done under cover of night will be done to you in the light of day. (See 2 Sam. 12:11-12.)

Finally, David learns of Absalom's plan to attack. With the help of Joab, his trusted general, he draws up a battle plan, insisting that the soldiers spare Absalom's life. David's forces win the battle, but Joab finds Absalom alone and kills him. David is grief-stricken at the death of another son and famously laments:

> O my son Absalom,
> Absalom my dear, dear son!
>
> *2 Samuel 19:1*

At this point, Joab tells David to snap out of his grief: "Get hold of yourself; get out there and put some heart into your servants! I swear to GOD that if you don't go to them they'll desert; not a soldier will be left here by nightfall. And that will be the worst thing that has happened yet" (2 Samuel 19:7). David agreed, and when the people saw him sitting at the gate, they came to him. They forgave and were reconciled to one another, and David returned to Jerusalem.

David gets back on track—as we need to do

There was one more threat. Absalom's brother Adonijah began plotting to become the next king. Some encouraged him, but Zadok the priest and Nathan the prophet were opposed. Nathan talked to Bathsheba and told her to remind David that he had promised the kingship to her son Solomon. David agreed, and Solomon was crowned just as Adonijah and his followers were having a banquet. The rebels finally gave up.

The Bible records the last instructions of David to his son Solomon. They seem most appropriate for our own times.

> *I'm about to go the way of all the earth, but you—be strong; show what you're made of! Do what GOD tells you. Walk in the paths he shows you: Follow the life-map absolutely, keep an eye out for the signposts, his course for life set out in the revelation to Moses; then you'll get on well in whatever you do and wherever you go. Then GOD will confirm what he prom-*

ised me when he said, "If your sons watch their step, staying true to me heart and soul, you'll always have a successor on Israel's throne."

1 Kings 2:1-3

David's sin of adultery and attempted cover-up certainly resonates with our own times. Our culture is saturated with sexual enticements. Men and women mingle freely, and sexual encounters are encouraged more than in previous generations. For many, sex has lost its specialness and its sacredness. It is just another form of recreation. Pornographic images are easily available. Men who want to follow God's plan for human sexuality will be tested regularly. The David/Bathsheba story unmasks the human tendency to rationalize sinful behavior. All of us need a combination of regular prayer, self-honesty, and avoidance of sexually-charged situations if we are going to lead sexually responsible lives.

At the same time, the story reveals the truth that sin does not have to be the final word. Repentance and forgiveness are always available to us. David's acts of contrition and appeals to God's mercy reveal his basic spiritual nature. Like him, we can recover from sinful lapses, learn important lessons, and move forward with our lives.

Sin does not have to be the final word.

Finally, the rebellion of Absalom must have been a terribly disappointing experience for David. Any parent who has had to deal with a rebellious child can empathize with him. Parents are torn between wanting to discipline their children and trying to maintain their love for them. Sometimes counseling—individual or family—can help. We must not be ashamed to seek help through the resources available to us. At other times, a combination of prayer and tough love can bring about healing and reconciliation. A loving and disciplined family life is still the best way to form healthy, productive, and caring children for the next generation.

QUESTIONS FOR REFLECTION AND DISCUSSION

1. David had a difficult relationship with Saul, but he always maintained his respect for him. What leadership roles have you been called to? Whom did you have to replace? How did you prepare yourself to do so?

2. Instead of trying to cover up, what do you think David should have done when he learned that Bathsheba was pregnant with his child? Have you ever tried to cover something up? Without giving details, what was the result?

3. In response to Nathan's confrontation, David could have tried to justify his actions. What do you think helped him to admit and repent? Do you have anything that you need to get off your chest? How and when will you do so?

4. What are some of the lessons you have learned from your own mistakes and moral lapses?

5. What is the role of art and music in your life? How does it connect with your spirituality?

ELIJAH

A Prophet Who Wouldn't Give Up

The Bible often links Moses and Elijah together under the title of "The Law and the Prophets." For example, in the story of the Transfiguration of Jesus, Moses and Elijah were the two depicted as meeting and discussing with Jesus on a mountaintop. (See Matthew 17:1-13.)

Moses is remembered as the one through whom God established his covenant with the people of Israel and gave them the Ten Commandments and other wise laws to guide their relationships with God and their neighbors.

Elijah stands at the top of the list of prophets. Prophecy in the Scriptures is not so much a matter of *foretelling the future* as it is of *speaking on behalf of God*. The prophet, both by words and actions, proclaims God's will for the people and calls them back to the commitments they made to live according to God's commandments.

Elijah starts with compassion—which is a good place for us to start as well

Elijah's name is significant; it means "The Lord (Yahweh) is my God." Elijah was sent by God thousands of years ago to challenge those Israelites who were fascinated by the worship of the pagan gods of the people around them, especially the god Baal. Ahab, the king of Israel, had married a pagan woman named Jezebel, who had introduced the worship of Baal to the Jewish people. We first meet Elijah when he tells Ahab that a severe drought is about to come upon the land of Israel. Then God tells Elijah to withdraw to a place east of the Jordan River, where ravens supplied him with food and he could drink from a nearby stream.

But, after a time, the stream runs dry, and God orders Elijah to move to a town in Sidon, where a widow, whom he did not know, would provide for him. Elijah meets the woman as she was gathering some sticks and asks her to bring him a cup of water and some bread. She confesses that she is down to her last bit of flour and oil; she is gathering sticks to bake one last meal for herself and her young son, after which they will both surely die.

> She said, "I swear, as surely as your GOD lives, I don't have so much as a biscuit. I have a handful of flour in a jar and a little oil in a bottle; you found me scratching together just enough firewood to make a last meal for my son and me. After we eat it, we'll die."
>
> Elijah said to her, "Don't worry about a thing. Go ahead and do what you've said. But first make a small biscuit for me and bring it back here. Then go ahead and make a meal from what's left for you and your son. This is the word of the GOD of Israel: 'The jar of flour will not run out and the bottle of oil will not become empty before GOD sends rain on the land and ends this drought.'"
>
> And she went right off and did it, did just as Elijah asked. And it turned out as he said—daily food for her and her family. The jar of meal didn't run out and the bottle of oil didn't become empty: GOD's promise fulfilled to the letter, exactly as Elijah had delivered it!
>
> *1 Kings 17:12-16*

The widow did exactly as Elijah told her. Sure enough: she, her son, and Elijah were able to eat for a whole year until the drought was ended.

One of the lessons here, as repeated many other places in the Bible, including the New Testament, is that God is a God of abundance, not scarcity. If we have faith, even as tiny as a mustard seed Jesus said, we will all flourish. What is the story of the feeding of the multitude if it is not that if we share what we have and work together, we can survive? This is not some kind of "Gospel of Prosperity" that says if we believe we automatically become rich. Rather it is a statement about the nature of God, who only gives good things, which we can all access when we follow the law of love of God and love of neighbor.

Sometime later, the woman's son became desperately ill and actually stopped breathing. She complained to Elijah, practically blaming him for the sickness. So Elijah took the boy upstairs and prayed:

> "GOD, my God, put breath back into this boy's body!" GOD listened to Elijah's prayer and put breath back into his body— he was alive! Elijah picked the boy up, carried him downstairs from the loft, and gave him to his mother. "Here's your son," said Elijah, "alive!"
>
> The woman said to Elijah, "I see it all now—you are a holy man. When you speak, GOD speaks—a true word!"
>
> 1 Kings 17:21-24

It is interesting to note that, of all the Old Testament prophets, Elijah is the only one who possessed miraculous powers.

Elijah takes on the bad guys—as we all have to do sometimes

Elijah learned that king Ahab was looking for him, and he knew this meant trouble. He took it upon himself to travel to the king personally, but he forced the king to come out to meet him.

> The moment Ahab saw Elijah he said, "So it's you, old trouble-maker!"
>
> "It's not I who has caused trouble in Israel," said Elijah, "but you and your government—you've dumped GOD's ways and

commands and run off after the local gods, the Baals. Here's
what I want you to do: Assemble everyone in Israel at Mount
Carmel. And make sure that the special pets of Jezebel, the
four hundred and fifty prophets of the local gods, the Baals,
and the four hundred prophets of the whore goddess Asherah,
are there."

1 Kings 18:17-19

So Elijah is no coward. No prophet is, although they often struggle to overcome their fear. Here, Elijah is not only calling out the king and "the special pets of Jezebel"—450 prophets of the local god, Baal, and the 400 prophets of "the whore goddess," Asherah. By my count, that is 850-1. The test will be which side can light a fire with no match.

The prophets of Baal call upon their god from morning till noon. But there is no sound and no fire. Then they began to hop around the altar, while Elijah taunted them, "Call a little louder—he is a god, after all. Maybe he's off meditating somewhere or other, or maybe he's gotten involved in a project, or maybe he's on vacation. You don't suppose he's overslept, do you, and needs to be waked up?" (1 Kings 18:27). Besides being brave, Elijah also has a sense of humor.

The next scene is one of the most dramatic in the whole Bible. Elijah places twelve stones representing the twelve tribes of Israel in the form of an altar. Then he digs a trench all around it and places the animal pieces upon it. He has the people pour water over the meat and over the wood—not once but three times—till everything is soaked and the trench is full of water. Then Elijah prays aloud to God: "O GOD, God of Abraham, Isaac, and Israel, make it known right now that you are God in Israel, that I am your servant, and that I'm doing what I'm doing under your orders. Answer me, GOD; O answer me and reveal to this people that you are GOD, the true God, and that you are giving these people another chance at repentance" (1 Kings 18:36-37). Talk about putting your reputation on the line! Elijah put it out there, trusting God to come through.

Suddenly, fire came down from heaven, consumed both the sacrifice and the altar, and lapped up the water in the trench. Seeing this, all the people fell prostrate and said, "God is the true God! God is the true God!" (1 Kings 18:39)

Elijah gets scared, then gets his courage back— just like we do

So, Elijah won the contest. But when Ahab's wife Jezebel heard about this, she was furious and sent a messenger to Elijah with a death threat. So Elijah, despite his courage, fled to the desert and sat down beneath a broom tree, which is a shrub-like tree in the deserts of Palestine that can grow as tall as 10-12 feet and is often the only shade available for travelers. Hence, it symbolizes renewal.

Maybe Elijah felt he had bitten off more than he could chew. Or maybe he had expected everyone to come over to his side with the one demonstration of God's power. In any case, a heavy sadness overcame him, and he prayed for death: "Enough of this, GOD! Take my life—I'm ready to join my ancestors in the grave!" (1 Kings 19:4).

Elijah fell asleep under the broom tree, but an angel woke him up and told him to eat and drink; there was a hearth cake and a jug of water next to him. He fell asleep again, but again the angel woke him and told him to move on. This time he obeyed; he walked through desert country until he came to Mt. Sinai, the very place where God first made the covenant and gave the commandments to Moses and the Israelites.

Elijah took shelter in a cave. But God spoke to him, asking him what he was doing there. Elijah poured out his heart to God: "'I've been working my heart out for the GOD-of-the-Angel-Armies,' said Elijah. 'The people of Israel have abandoned your covenant, destroyed the places of worship, and murdered your prophets. I'm the only one left, and now they're trying to kill me'" (1 Kings 19:10). As we would probably say today, "I just can't take it anymore!"

Then God told him to stand at the entrance to the cave and wait for the Lord to pass by. As Elijah stood there, a mighty wind began to crush rocks on the mountain; this was followed by an earthquake, then by fire. But God's presence was not in any of these natural phenomena. Finally, Elijah heard "a gentle and quiet whisper" (1 Kings 19:12), and it was then he experienced the sacred presence of God. This is a lesson for those of us who want to experience God in some emotional, mystical encounter. It usually doesn't work that way. All most of us get is a tiny whisper so we had better listen carefully.

Elijah heard God say to him: your work is not finished: go back to your people. Anoint Jehu as king for Israel; he is a good man. Anoint Elisha as prophet to succeed you; he too is a good man. In fact, there are still 7,000 good people in Israel who have not gone over to the god Baal. They need you, Elijah. They need your faith, your leadership, your encouragement. Don't let them down. Elijah obeyed, returned to the land of Israel and fulfilled the mandates God had given him. (See 1 Kings 19:15-18.)

Elijah mentors his successor—as we sometimes do

Elijah went in search of Elisha in order to call him to the ministry of prophet. Elisha asked permission to take leave of his family first, and Elijah agreed. Next, God told Elijah to confront King Ahab for his blatantly unjust seizure of a citizen's vineyard and his subsequent murder; the man's name was Naboth. Indeed, the Bible notes this terrible indictment of Ahab: "Ahab, pushed by his wife Jezebel and in open defiance of GOD, set an all-time record in making big business of evil" (1 Kings 21:25). So, Elijah challenged Ahab on his evil ways and promised that the Lord would deal out severe punishments on him and his family. Ahab was stricken with fear and went into a penitential mode: "When Ahab heard what Elijah had to say, he ripped his clothes to shreds, dressed in penitential rough burlap, and fasted. He even slept in coarse burlap pajamas. He tiptoed around, quiet as a mouse" (1 Kings 21:26). As a result, God spared Ahab and reserved the most serious punishments for his son Ahaziah, who turned out to be an even worse king than Ahab.

Meanwhile, Elijah was mentoring Elisha and preparing him to succeed as prophet in Israel. As they were traveling along and came to Bethel, one of Israel's sanctuaries, Elijah told Elisha to stay there while he continued on. However, Elisha said he would not leave him. They continued on until they came to Jericho. Again Elijah told Elisha to stay behind, but Elisha refused. Finally, they came to the river Jordan, which was too deep to cross. Elijah rolled up his mantle and struck the water with it. The water divided, and they were able to cross over. (Note the parallels with Moses.) Then Elijah said to Elisha:

"What can I do for you before I'm taken from you? Ask anything."

Elisha said, "Your life repeated in my life. I want to be a holy man just like you."

"That's a hard one!" said Elijah. "But if you're watching when I'm taken from you, you'll get what you've asked for. But only if you're watching."

And so it happened. They were walking along and talking. Suddenly a chariot and horses of fire came between them and Elijah went up in a whirlwind to heaven. Elisha saw it all and shouted, "My father, my father! You—the chariot and cavalry of Israel!" When he could no longer see anything, he grabbed his robe and ripped it to pieces. Then he picked up Elijah's cloak that had fallen from him, returned to the shore of the Jordan, and stood there. He took Elijah's cloak—all that was left of Elijah!—and hit the river with it, saying, "Now where is the GOD of Elijah? Where is he?"

When he struck the water, the river divided and Elisha walked through.

The guild of prophets from Jericho saw the whole thing from where they were standing. They said, "The spirit of Elijah lives in Elisha!" They welcomed and honored him.

2 Kings 2:9-15

Because of the scene of Elijah going "up to heaven in a whirl-wind," a tradition grew up among the Jewish people that Elijah would return to earth and complete his prophetic mission. Jesus himself noted this after his transfiguration when Moses and Elijah appeared with him on a mountain. The apostles who were with him asked about the return of Elijah:

Jesus answered, "Elijah does come and get everything ready. I'm telling you, Elijah has already come but they didn't know him when they saw him. They treated him like dirt, the same way they are about to treat the Son of Man." That's when the disciples realized that all along he had been talking about John the Baptizer.

Matthew 17:11-13

It has been said that every generation needs prophets. Human beings can too easily lose sight of truths and values that hold societies together. When a nation or a people are drifting toward self-absorption or national amnesia, prophets hold up a mirror and say, "Look at yourselves! Can't you see what's happening?" They call us to return to those beliefs and values that made us great. At other times, of course, they may reveal to us that some of our former ways of thinking and acting are indeed outmoded, and there is need for major change. In any case, prophets usually have a double function: they make us uncomfortable, but they also give us hope. Think of figures like Martin Luther King, Dorothy Day, Mother Teresa, Thomas Merton, and the new twin papal saints, John XXIII and John Paul II.

It's good to note that Elijah began his ministry with acts of compassion, not prophecy. He helped the widow and her son to survive through the terrible drought, then he raised her son from death or near-death. His time spent in seclusion purified him from any delusions of self-importance or glory-seeking. He was now ready for the hard and unappreciated work of confronting the people on their idolatries.

We are called to be prophets, maybe with a small "p."

Who do we regard as prophets in our own time? We should not listen to every voice in our culture that clamors for our hearing. Pop stars, movie and TV stars, and sports stars can hardly classify as prophets. Sometimes, of course, the words of a song, a well-written book, movie, or play can provide a prophetic message, either of challenge or of hope. But, we need to carefully choose the voices we listen to.

At the same time, we are called to be prophets, maybe with a small "p." At our baptism, we were anointed with holy oil and told that we are to be "priests, prophets, and kings"—visible images of Christ in our world. We are prophetic when we speak up for the rights of the unborn; when we ask our legislators to provide more funding for the poor and less for destructive weapons; when we refuse to lie or cover up for illegal or immoral practices in the workplace; when we gently but firmly correct others who use foul language or denigrate other people.

Another connection: like Elijah, we are sometimes tempted to "lie under a broom tree" in self-pity when our efforts to make the world a better place are ignored, opposed, or even ridiculed. We just want to quit. God understands that feeling. But, we need to listen to the angelic voice that bids us get up and continue the journey. God usually does not break rocks or make lightning flashes to get our attention. Rather, we find him in a tiny whispering sound that comes to us in quiet moments—if we are listening.

Finally, there is deep symbolism in Elisha's picking up the cloak that fell from the shoulders of Elijah. Sometimes we are like Elisha—asked to pick up and continue the task, the project, the mission that somebody else has begun. There is dignity and great meaning in that, even though we may not be recognized or appreciated for it. Other times, we are more like Elijah: called to be mentors for those coming after us. This may take a literal form, such as acting as a role model for young people, including our own children or grandchildren, or participating in a structured mentoring program for people at work or in the community. We are then handing over the mantle so others may thrive and grow through our influence and we can get out of the way. That is a life-giving endeavor indeed.

QUESTIONS FOR DISCUSSION AND REFLECTION

1. Who are some of the "prophets" who have helped form your own ideals and life-values? Offer a prayer for them now.

2. Think of a situation in your own life when you were tempted to quit some project or endeavor. How did you deal with it? What did you learn from it?

3. Have you ever been a mentor for someone? What was that experience like?

4. What is the relationship between fear and courage? How do you overcome one to find the other? Give some examples.

5. When do you best hear the "gentle quiet whisper" of God?

JEREMIAH

A Man Unbeaten
by Depression and Failure

Here is a great man of the Bible who suffered from severe depression and self-doubt, yet was able to overcome it. Jeremiah was born around 645 B.C. in a small village near Jerusalem, toward the end of the 45-year reign of King Manasseh (687-642 B.C.). The king had become notorious for his evil policies: fostering paganism and idolatry, practicing immorality and political corruption, and oppressing the poor. The new king, Josiah, had instituted a wide-ranging movement of political and spiritual reform aimed at returning the kingdom of Judah to the worship of God and observance of the Mosaic Law.

When he was only about 18, Jeremiah received a clear call from God to become his prophet and support the reforms of Josiah. At first, he protested, saying that he was too young and inarticulate to be a prophet. But the Lord answered in a very famous passage of the Bible that we all know:

> *Before I shaped you in the womb,*
> *I knew all about you.*
> *Before you saw the light of day,*
> *I had holy plans for you:*
> *A prophet to the nations—*
> *that's what I had in mind for you.*
>
> *Jeremiah 1:5*

As was done with the prophet Isaiah before him, God touched Jeremiah's mouth and then said:

> *Look! I've just put my words in your mouth—hand-delivered!*
> *See what I've done? I've given you a job to do*
> *among nations and governments—a red-letter day!*
> *Your job is to pull up and tear down,*
> *take apart and demolish,*
> *And then start over,*
> *building and planting.*
>
> Jeremiah 1:9-10

Jeremiah tells it like it is— as we sometimes have to do

Jeremiah began his prophetic ministry by calling upon the people to wake up, to realize how far they had fallen away from God. He urged them to return to God by following the reforms of King Josiah. He had some success at first. One of the scribes, Ezra, had discovered a scroll of the book of Deuteronomy hidden in the Jerusalem temple. The priests called all the people together and read from the scroll from morning till noon. The people were stunned: "We have not been living this way," they said in effect, "it is time to return to the Lord." (See Nehemiah 8:1-12.) But not everyone was in the mood for reform. So Jeremiah continued confronting the people:

> *Hear GOD's Message, House of Jacob!*
> *Yes, you—House of Israel!*
> *GOD's Message: "What did your ancestors find fault with in me*
> *that they drifted so far from me,*
> *Took up with Sir Windbag*
> *and turned into windbags themselves?*
>
> *It never occurred to them to say, 'Where's GOD,*
> *the God who got us out of Egypt,*

Who took care of us through thick and thin,
*   those rough-and-tumble*
*   wilderness years of parched deserts and death valleys,*
A land that no one who enters comes out of,
*   a cruel, inhospitable land?'*
                                        Jeremiah 2:4-6

Try to imagine the courage it must have taken for young Jeremiah to utter this stinging rebuke from God to his elders. Imagine it was some young adult in your life right now saying something like this to the people of your parish:

My people have committed a compound sin:
*   they've walked out on me, the fountain*
Of fresh flowing waters, and then dug cisterns—
*   cisterns that leak, cisterns that are no better than sieves.*
                                        Jeremiah 2:13

Jeremiah makes the consequences clear— and so must we

The new superpower in the region at the time was Babylon. They had inflicted severe defeats on the Assyrians in the north; meanwhile, Egypt invaded Israel from the south to stop the Babylonians. King Josiah tried to fight them but was killed in battle. Egypt took over all of Palestine and replaced Josiah with their own puppet, Jehoiakim, as king. He revived the pagan practices and became puffed up with his own importance. At one point, Jeremiah denounced him for building his fine cedar home on the backs of the poor, speaking for God:

"Doom to him who builds palaces but bullies people,
*   who makes a fine house but destroys lives,*
Who cheats his workers
*   and won't pay them for their work,*

Who says, 'I'll build me an elaborate mansion
with spacious rooms and fancy windows.
I'll bring in rare and expensive woods
and the latest in interior decor.'
So, that makes you a king—
living in a fancy palace?"

Jeremiah 22: 13-14

Jeremiah even had the gall to challenge the people in the Temple itself. Don't keep coming here to worship, he said in the words of God, unless you intend to reform your ways: "Only if you clean up your act (the way you live, the things you do), only if you do a total spring cleaning on the way you live and treat your neighbors, only if you quit exploiting the street people and orphans and widows, no longer taking advantage of innocent people on this very site and no longer destroying your souls by using this Temple as a front for other gods—only *then* will I move into your neighborhood. Only then will this country I gave your ancestors be my permanent home, my Temple" (Jeremiah 7:5-7). Jeremiah drove the point home with this powerful indictment in the words of the Lord: "You are the nation that wouldn't obey GOD, that refused all discipline. Truth has disappeared. There's not a trace of it left in your mouths" (Jeremiah 7:28).

Jeremiah's words and actions certainly resonate with our own times. Our society, it seems, is drifting further away from its religious and moral foundations. The gods of money, pleasure, and power are replacing the true God in the minds and hearts of many. "Palace-building" now takes the form of luxurious mansions and stock portfolios. Like the people of Jeremiah's time, even Christians who pray, read the Bible, and attend church regularly may continue to disregard God's commandments and neglect the poor and suffering people around them.

Jeremiah complained that even the idea of telling the truth had disappeared from the people's vocabulary. "There's not a trace of it left in your mouths." It makes me think of some of the radio and television talk shows that fill the air today.

Isn't it true that some other words have also vanished from our speech today? *Faithfulness* seems like one of them. *Innocence* is another, especially when it comes to moral behavior. To be seen as innocent is not cool. Same with *reverence*. It seems that any comedian has to be *ir-reverent* if he or she going to be popular. You can probably think of other words that appear to be fading from our speech.

Jeremiah experiences inner struggles— as we all do

As Jeremiah continued to challenge the people and the power structure of his time, he aroused the antagonism of many around him and they began to oppose him. He brought his complaint to God in prayer:

> *You are right, O GOD, and you set things right.*
> *I can't argue with that. But I do have some questions:*
> *Why do bad people have it so good?*
> *Why do con artists make it big?*
> *You planted them and they put down roots.*
> *They flourished and produced fruit.*
> *They talk as if they're old friends with you,*
> *but they couldn't care less about you.*
> *Meanwhile, you know me inside and out.*
> *You don't let me get by with a thing!*

> *Jeremiah 12:1-2*

God's answer was chilling and challenging: "So, Jeremiah, if you're worn out in this footrace with men, what makes you think you can race against horses? And if you can't keep your wits during times of calm, what's going to happen when troubles break loose like the Jordan in flood?" (Jeremiah 12:5). As St. Teresa of Avila once said to God, "If this is how you treat your friends, no wonder you have so few of them!" Later we see Jeremiah slipping into depression. He again complains over and over to God. Here is the answer he received:

> *Take back those words, and I'll take you back.*
> > *Then you'll stand tall before me.*
> *Use words truly and well. Don't stoop to cheap whining.*
> > *Then, but only then, you'll speak for me.*
> *Let your words change them.*
> > *Don't change your words to suit them.*
> *I'll turn you into a steel wall,*
> > *a thick steel wall, impregnable.*
> *They'll attack you but won't put a dent in you*
> > *because I'm at your side, defending and delivering....*
> *I'll deliver you from the grip of the wicked.*
> > *I'll get you out of the clutch of the ruthless."*

Jeremiah 15:19-21

As I mentioned earlier, God's words "I'll be with you" appear numerous times in the Bible. God never promises to protect us from all trouble and suffering, but that we will not be abandoned and will ultimately prevail—but only if we remain faithful. But that truth has to be learned again and again. So a few chapters later, God instructs Jeremiah to buy a potter's clay flask, go the city gate, gather people together, and then smash the flask saying, "Listen to God's Word, you kings of Judah and people of Jerusalem! This is the Message from God-of-the-Angel-Armies, the God of Israel. I'm about to bring doom crashing down on this place" (Jeremiah 19:3). Not exactly the kind of proclamation that is going to endear him to his neighbors!

When the chief of the temple police, Pashur, heard about this action, he arrested Jeremiah, had him scourged, put him in the stocks overnight, and released him in the morning. Jeremiah says to him:

> *"God has a new name for you: not Pashur but Danger-Everywhere, because God says, 'You're a danger to yourself and everyone around you. All your friends are going to get killed*

in battle while you stand there and watch. What's more, I'm turning all of Judah over to the king of Babylon to do whatever he likes with them—haul them off into exile, kill them at whim. Everything worth anything in this city, property and possessions along with everything in the royal treasury—I'm handing it all over to the enemy. They'll rummage through it and take what they want back to Babylon. And you, Pashur, you and everyone in your family will be taken prisoner into exile—that's right, exile in Babylon. You'll die and be buried there, you and all your cronies to whom you preached your lies.'"

Jeremiah 20:3-6

Jeremiah complains to God—as do we sometimes

As we can imagine, Pashur and the other leaders and all the people were furious with Jeremiah. He was basically threatening them with destruction of their way of life and exile from their country. At this point, Jeremiah again pours out his complaints to God in the strongest possible language:

You pushed me into this, God, and I let you do it.
    You were too much for me.
And now I'm a public joke.
    They all poke fun at me.
Every time I open my mouth
    I'm shouting, "Murder!" or "Rape!"
And all I get for my God-warnings
    are insults and contempt.
But if I say, "Forget it!
    No more God-Messages from me!"
The words are fire in my belly,
    a burning in my bones.
I'm worn out trying to hold it in.
    I can't do it any longer!

Jeremiah 20:7-9

As someone once said, "No one could be more alone in spirit than Jeremiah at the moment of this prayer." He has nowhere to turn but back to God with trust. "But GOD, a most fierce warrior, is at my side. Those who are after me will be sent sprawling—slapstick buffoons falling all over themselves, a spectacle of humiliation no one will ever forget" (Jeremiah 20:11). Abraham Lincoln remarked, "I have been driven to my knees more often than not by the sheer realization that I had nowhere else to go."

In 605 B.C., the Babylonians drove the Egyptians out of northern Palestine. They demanded tribute from King Jehoiakim, but he refused. A couple years later, under King Nebuchadnezzar, the Babylonians began a siege of Jerusalem, and the city fell into their hands in 597. Jehoiakim was taken captive into exile, and the Babylonians set up Zedekiah as a puppet king. For a few years, Zedekiah submitted to their rule, but then he began a rebellion and Nebuchadnezzar besieged Jerusalem again. Zedekiah sent his priests to ask Jeremiah what would happen. "Will God once again spare us as he did in 701 when the Assyrians tried to capture the holy city?" "No," said Jeremiah. "Your army will be beaten, the citizens will die by the sword and famine, and the city will be burned with fire. Therefore, tell the people and the army to surrender, not fight; it will be better for everyone." God is using Nebuchadnezzar to punish Israel for its infidelity.

But the king and the people would hear none of it. They tried to resist, but it was useless. In 587, Nebuchadnezzar's army broke through the city walls. They destroyed most of the city, including the magnificent Temple that Solomon had built, killed many of the inhabitants, and took a large number as captives into Babylon, including King Zedekiah. He had to watch as his two sons were executed, and then his own eyes were gouged out. It was the lowest point in the history of Israel. The brief Book of Lamentations, which follows Jeremiah in the Bible, depicts the heart-rending suffering of the people who remained in Jerusalem after its capture, as well as their determination not to give up hope:

I gave up on life altogether.
   I've forgotten what the good life is like.
I said to myself, "This is it. I'm finished.
   God is a lost cause."
I'll never forget the trouble, the utter lostness,
   the taste of ashes, the poison I've swallowed.
I remember it all—oh, how well I remember—
   the feeling of hitting the bottom.
But there's one other thing I remember,
   and remembering, I keep a grip on hope:

God's loyal love couldn't have run out,
   his merciful love couldn't have dried up.
They're created new every morning.
   How great your faithfulness!
I'm sticking with God (I say it over and over).
   He's all I've got left.

Lamentations 3:17-24

Jeremiah gets his second wind—as we will too

Amazingly, shortly after this terrible disaster, Jeremiah had a prophetic vision of the Messiah to come, which he delivered in God's voice. The Catholic Church uses this text at the beginning of every Advent season to remind us that Jesus is the fulfillment of this prophecy:

"Time's coming"—God's Decree—
   "when I'll establish a truly righteous David-Branch,
A ruler who knows how to rule justly.
   He'll make sure of justice and keep people united.
In his time Judah will be secure again
   and Israel will live in safety.
This is the name they'll give him:
   'God-Who-Puts-Everything-Right.'"

Jeremiah 23:5-6

Jeremiah also wrote a letter to the exiles, telling them God wanted them to settle in for the long haul; they will be in Babylon for about seventy years. God wanted them to build houses, plant gardens, marry wives so that their numbers would increase rather than decrease. "Make yourselves at home there and work for the country's welfare. Pray for Babylon's well-being. If things go well for Babylon, things will go well for you" (Jeremiah 29:7). Then Jeremiah adds God's beautiful promise:

"As soon as Babylon's seventy years are up and not a day before, I'll show up and take care of you as I promised and bring you back home. I know what I'm doing. I have it all planned out—plans to take care of you, not abandon you, plans to give you the future you hope for.

"When you call on me, when you come and pray to me, I'll listen.

"When you come looking for me, you'll find me.

"Yes, when you get serious about finding me and want it more than anything else, I'll make sure you won't be disappointed." GOD's Decree.

"I'll turn things around for you. I'll bring you back from all the countries into which I drove you"—GOD's Decree—"bring you home to the place from which I sent you off into exile. You can count on it."

Jeremiah 29:10-14

We can only imagine the comfort these words brought to the Jewish exiles in Babylon. Jeremiah went on to foretell the eventual return of the exiles and the rebuilding of Jerusalem. He also prophesied that God will one day form a new covenant with the Israelites:

"'The time is coming when I will make a brand-new covenant with Israel and Judah. It won't be a repeat of the covenant I made with their ancestors when I took their hand to lead them out of the land of Egypt. They broke that covenant even

though I did my part as their Master.' GOD's Decree. 'This is
the brand-new covenant that I will make with Israel when
the time comes. I will put my law within them—write it on
their hearts!—and be their God. And they will be my people.
They will no longer go around setting up schools to teach each
other about GOD. They'll know me firsthand, the dull and the
bright, the smart and the slow. I'll wipe the slate clean for each
of them. I'll forget they ever sinned!' GOD's Decree."

Jeremiah 31:31-33

Christians believe that Jesus fulfilled this prophecy when he inaugurated the New Covenant at the Last Supper on the night before he died.

After the city of Jerusalem was destroyed, many of the remaining inhabitants wanted to flee to Egypt. They asked Jeremiah to pray and consult the Lord. After ten days, Jeremiah gave his answer. This is what the Lord God says: "If you remain here quietly, I will build you up; you will not have to fear the king of Babylon, for I am with you to save you." However, the Lord says, "If you have determined to go to Egypt and make that your home, then the very wars you fear will catch up with you in Egypt and the starvation you dread will track you down in Egypt. You'll die there! Every last one of you who is determined to go to Egypt and make it your home will either be killed, starve, or get sick and die. No survivors, not one! No one will escape the doom that I'll bring upon you" (Jeremiah 42:16-17).

But the leaders decided to go anyway, and they forced Jeremiah to accompany them. He died in Egypt of natural causes some three years later, around the year 580 B.C. On the surface, he was a failure in every way, but we cannot help but admire the courage of Jeremiah. He never wanted to be a prophet in the first place; but when God called, him he obeyed. In our own life, we sometimes know that we ought to speak up for something we strongly believe in, or challenge some attitude or behavior we know is wrong— even if it will mean criticism or rejection from others. This requires the virtue of fortitude, which is also one of the gifts of the Holy Spirit. We see it in people who pray outside abortion clinics and adopt children who might have been aborted or would otherwise have no family; who challenge their employers on unethical practices; who refuse to lie for someone who faces trouble for irresponsible actions. We see it in young people who resist peer pressure to indulge in drug use or excessive drinking, or engage in sinful sexual activity; who agree to spend a year or two in volunteer service before beginning their careers. It is always inspiring when we learn about courageous actions like these.

> Speaking up for something we believe in requires the virtue of fortitude.

Another theme in Jeremiah's life is depression, something which affects a significant number of men today. Depression is sometimes situational; it arises from the experience of loss—of a job, money, a valued relationship, an illness or injury, respect or esteem from others, a loved one in death. This kind of depression generally lifts with the passage of time and with the loving support of other people. Sometimes, however, depression is caused by some kind of chemical imbalance in the brain or nervous system. In these cases, counseling and anti-depressant medication can usually bring relief. Finding help for depression is not a cause for shame.

Also, like Jeremiah, we need not be ashamed if we sometimes complain to God about the trials that are dragging us down. God understands that our endurance is sometimes exhausted. But then, like Jeremiah, we need to move beyond complaining—to ask for God's strength and comfort, and to renew our trust and confidence in his promise: "I will be with you. I will not abandon you."

We saw how Jeremiah sometimes slipped into feelings of personal failure. It is true that he did not succeed in turning the people away from their sinful ways and back to the honor and worship of the true God. Nor did he prevent some of his people from fleeing to Egypt, even forcing him to go with them. But he never let the fear of failure turn him away from his mission. He continued to speak the truth to a people who resisted hearing it. That ought to be our commitment as well: to keep doing what we know is right, regardless of the outcome. As Mother Teresa put it so well, "I never hear Jesus in the Gospels talking about success—only about faithfulness in loving."

Finally, I found a very personal connection in one of Jeremiah's experiences. At one point, God told him to write down for King Jehoiakim words of warning of the evils that will come upon the nation if the people do not reform their ways. So, Jeremiah dictated God's words to the scribe Baruch, who wrote them down on a scroll. Then he told Baruch to gather the people of Jerusalem and the surrounding region to the Temple and read the words of the scroll, hoping they would turn away from their evil ways. Another scribe took the scroll and had it read before the king and his ministers. But Jehoiakim made a mockery of it: each time the scribe read three or four columns, the king cut the pages off and threw them into the fire: "Neither the king nor any of his officials showed the slightest twinge of conscience as they listened to the messages read" (Jeremiah 36:24). Jeremiah had to dictate all the words to Baruch again. The "Letter of Jeremiah" forms the sixth chapter of the Book of Baruch in the Bible.

While writing this book you have before you, I was working on the final chapter when suddenly my computer screen went blank. I could not move up or down and could not recover my document. Our order's IT consultant happened to be in town and tried to help, but he could not find the document either. I took the computer to Best Buy: no luck. My nephew is a computer geek. He tried for over two hours to retrieve it: nothing. (But he did add another program so that whatever I write is saved in two places!) At that point, I was ready to just abandon this book, but I decided not to do that. Luckily, I had saved the first four chapters on a flash drive, but I had simply neglected to keep doing that as I continued. So I just started to rewrite the next chapters. I really think the book is better because of my goof because I kept getting new ideas while rewriting. Anyway, I certainly could identify with Jeremiah and Baruch on this point. Maybe you can as well.

QUESTIONS FOR REFLECTION AND DISCUSSION

1. Have you ever agreed to take on some responsibility even though you didn't feel confident about it? Why did you agree—and how did it work out?

2. Have you ever had to confront a person or group because they were doing something wrong? How did you handle it—and what was the outcome?

3. How do you react when you feel God has let you down? Be specific.

4. Have you or one of your loved ones ever suffered from depression? What helped—or did not help?

5. Did you ever lose something and have to start all over? Tell the story and the lessons you learned.

JOHN THE BAPTIST

Man without Ego

The place of honor we hold for John the Baptist can be seen in two obvious ways. First, for most saints, the Church celebrates the day of their death or martyrdom. For John, we also celebrate the day of his birth. The only other one so honored is Mary, the mother of Jesus. Second, Jesus himself said about John:

> *"What did you expect when you went out to see him in the wild? A weekend camper? Hardly. What then? A sheik in silk pajamas? Not in the wilderness, not by a long shot. What then? A prophet? That's right, a prophet! Probably the best prophet you'll ever hear. He is the prophet that Malachi announced when he wrote, 'I'm sending my prophet ahead of you, to make the road smooth for you.'*
>
> *"Let me tell you what's going on here: No one in history surpasses John the Baptizer."*
>
>

Matthew 11:8-11

John's birth and vocation are miracles— as our ours

We have little biographical information about John. His father, Zechariah, belonged to a family of Jewish priests of the tribe of Levi who, twice each year were appointed to offer the sacrifice of incense at the evening prayer in the Temple. Of John's parents, Zechariah and Elizabeth, the Bible says, "Together they lived honorably before God, careful in keeping to the ways of the commandments and enjoying a clear conscience before God" (Luke 1:6). It also notes that both were "quite old" and "childless because Elizabeth could never conceive" (Luke 1:7). This would have been considered a great stigma in Jewish society at the time.

One day, it was Zechariah's "one turn in life to enter the sanctuary of God and burn incense" (Luke 1:9). While he was completely alone in the sanctuary:

> *Unannounced, an angel of God appeared just to the right of the altar of incense. Zachariah was paralyzed in fear.*
>
> *But the angel reassured him, "Don't fear, Zachariah. Your prayer has been heard. Elizabeth, your wife, will bear a son by you. You are to name him John. You're going to leap like a gazelle for joy, and not only you—many will delight in his birth. He'll achieve great stature with God.*
>
> *"He'll drink neither wine nor beer. He'll be filled with the Holy Spirit from the moment he leaves his mother's womb. He will turn many sons and daughters of Israel back to their God. He will herald God's arrival in the style and strength of Elijah, soften the hearts of parents to children, and kindle devout understanding among hardened skeptics—he'll get the people ready for God."*
>
> *Zachariah said to the angel, "Do you expect me to believe this? I'm an old man and my wife is an old woman."*
>
> *But the angel said, "I am Gabriel, the sentinel of God, sent especially to bring you this glad news. But because you won't believe me, you'll be unable to say a word until the day of your son's birth. Every word I've spoken to you will come true on time—God's time."*
>
> *Luke 1:11-20*

Meanwhile, outside the sanctuary, the people were wondering what was keeping Zechariah so long in the sanctuary. "When he came out and couldn't speak, they knew he had seen a vision.

He continued speechless and had to use sign language with the people" (Luke 1:22). When Zechariah returned home, the promise was fulfilled. Elizabeth conceived and proclaimed, "So, this is how God acts to remedy my unfortunate condition!" (Luke 1:25).

In due time, Elizabeth gave birth to her son, and the whole town rejoiced with her. Everyone assumed he would be named Zechariah, but Elizabeth said he would be called John. The neighbors were puzzled because none of their relatives had that name. So they turned to the father and asked him. Zechariah asked for a writing table and wrote: "His name is to be John" (Luke 1:63). At once he regained his power of speech and burst into a beautiful prayer that priests and religious recite every day at their morning prayer:

> Blessed be the Lord, the God of Israel;
>> he came and set his people free.
> He set the power of salvation in the center of our lives,
>> and in the very house of David his servant,
> Just as he promised long ago
>> through the preaching of his holy prophets.
>
> Luke 1:68-70

The first lesson we can learn from the life of John the Baptist is this: Sometimes we need to wait a long time for God's plans to unfold. In the time and Jewish culture of Zechariah and Elizabeth, childlessness was a cause for shame. People took very seriously the command of God to Adam and Eve to "be fertile and multiply." This was especially important for members of the ancestral line of David. After all, the Messiah was to come from this family. So, even though childlessness may be no one's fault, it was still seen as some kind of disgrace for a married couple. Zechariah and Elizabeth continued to pray, entrusting themselves to the care and will of God. We can only imagine their joy at the birth of their son. The name John in Hebrew means "gift of God." But then, imagine the disappointment of John's parents when he takes off for the desert and does not marry. No grandchildren. Truly, something new and mysterious is taking place among God's people.

How often in our lives have we had to wait, in darkness and confusion, for God to act in our lives, for our fervent prayers to be answered? And especially when the answer is not what we had prayed and hoped for? At that point we have only two choices: to become bitter and cynical, or to hold fast to our trust in God and in his mysterious designs. I often tell people: God always answers our prayers, but there are three possible answers: "Yes"; "Not yet" (as in the case of Zechariah and Elizabeth); and "I have a better plan." In the last case, we may not receive what we asked for, but God in his wisdom gives us something we needed even more although it may take us a long time to recognize that gift. We can never go wrong in asking God for what we think we need, but always with the attitude: "I surrender in trust to your holy will."

Surely one of the deepest disappointments of married couples is to be incapable of bearing children. Modern science and technology have found ways to help infertile couples, but these are not always effective. Another possibility is adoption, the wonderful choice of providing loving parents and a home for orphaned children. I have been privileged to come to know parents who have made this choice. It is a wonderful form of love. Still other childless parents have found ways to be life-giving in non-biological ways, for example, through various forms of care and service to others. The same can be true for people who remain single.

John grows up and finds his vocation — as we all have to do

The Bible says: "A deep, reverential fear settled over the neighborhood, and in all that Judean hill country people talked about nothing else. Everyone who heard about it took it to heart, wondering, "What will become of this child? Clearly, God has his hand in this" (Luke 1:65-66). Then we read that "The child grew up, healthy and spirited. He lived out in the desert until the day he made his prophetic debut in Israel" (Luke 1:80).

Some scholars say that John joined the community of a Jewish sect named the Essenes. These monk-like people were disheartened by what they saw as the laxity and lack of spiritual fervor among many of their fellow Jews, as well as their tendency to be infected by the pagan Roman culture around them. So they withdrew to the Judean desert around the Dead Sea. There they lived a communal life of prayer, fasting, and study of the Scriptures. (We think it was the Essenes who were responsible for copying and hiding the Dead Sea Scrolls, which were discovered only recently and have given us great insight into the Hebrew Scriptures.)

A good number of the Essenes apparently chose to remain celibate. Whether or not John actually joined this community, we know that he spent time in the desert. There he was filled with the passion and spiritual energy he needed to bring his people back to God and prepare them for the coming of the Messiah.

John is called "the Baptist" or "the Baptizer," but he could perhaps better be called "the Evangelist." Luke sets the stage for John's mission by giving us a snapshot of "Who's Who in Palestine." He names the Roman emperor, Tiberius Caesar; Pontius Pilate, the local Roman governor of Palestine; the four lesser "tetrarchs"—Jewish rulers over various parts of Palestine, and the two Jewish high priests, Annas and his son-in-law Caiaphas, who will have a major role in the death of Jesus. Then Luke adds:

John, out in the desert at the time, received a message from God. He went all through the country around the Jordan River preaching a baptism of life-change leading to forgiveness of sins, as described in the words of Isaiah the prophet:

> *Thunder in the desert!*
> *"Prepare God's arrival!*
> *Make the road smooth and straight!*
> *Every ditch will be filled in,*
> *Every bump smoothed out,*
> *The detours straightened out,*
> *All the ruts paved over.*

Everyone will be there to see
The parade of God's salvation."

Luke 3:3-6

John's basic message was this: Reform your lives; you've forgotten you are God's chosen and holy people. Just because the Romans have conquered you physically, don't let them dominate you spiritually. You've drifted into thinking, as they do, that the major goal of life is to become comfortable, acquire a high position, impress the right people. And you have pushed God off to the margin of your lives.

Before long, people were flocking to the river to hear John and to ask for baptism. But before he would do so, he had practical advice for each of the groups that came to him. To the religious leaders, he thundered: "Brood of snakes! What do you think you're doing slithering down here to the river? Do you think a little water on your snakeskins is going to deflect God's judgment? It's your *life* that must change, not your skin. And don't think you can pull rank by claiming Abraham as 'father.' Being a child of Abraham is neither here nor there—children of Abraham are a dime a dozen. God can make children from stones if he wants. What counts is your life. Is it green and blossoming? Because if it's deadwood, it goes on the fire" (Luke 3:7-9). To the tax collectors, John said: "Stop cheating the people by demanding more than they owe and pocketing the difference for yourselves." To the soldiers: "Do not practice extortion and do not falsely accuse anyone." To the ordinary Jewish person: "If you have extra food and clothing, share them with those who are needy."

John gives way to Jesus—as we must too

One day Jesus himself, John's cousin, came to the river and asked for baptism. John objected at first, saying that he ought to be baptized by Jesus, not the other way around. But when Jesus insisted, John complied, just as we must do when Jesus insists! After the baptism, John testified:

> "I watched the Spirit, like a dove flying down out of the sky, making himself at home in him. I repeat, I know nothing about him except this: The One who authorized me to baptize with water told me, 'The One on whom you see the Spirit come down and stay, this One will baptize with the Holy Spirit.' That's exactly what I saw happen, and I'm telling you, there's no question about it: This is the Son of God."
>
> *John 1:32-34*

I titled this chapter "John the Baptist: Man without Ego." He clearly enjoyed great success at first, as people flocked to him from all over the country. But soon the Jewish members of the Pharisee party began to challenge him, saying, "Who are you anyway?" Probably the intent was: "Who do you think you are!" They could not fathom a man who had not studied and had no credentials calling people to be baptized as a sign that they intended to reform their lives spiritually. John dismissed all the usual opinions: "I am not the Messiah...not Elijah...not the Prophet." "Well, who then?" they insisted. John's answer:

> "A person you don't recognize has taken his stand in your midst. He comes after me, but he is not in second place to me. I'm not even worthy to hold his coat for him."
>
> *John 1:27*

Then, the very next day, John saw Jesus coming toward him and yelled out:

> "Here he is, God's Passover Lamb! He forgives the sins of the world! This is the man I've been talking about, 'the One who comes after me but is really ahead of me.' I knew nothing about who he was—only this: that my task has been to get Israel ready to recognize him as the God-Revealer. That is why I came here baptizing with water, giving you a good bath and scrubbing sins from your life so you can get a fresh start with God."
>
> *John 1:29-31*

John did not even try to hold on to his own disciples; he was eager to turn them to Jesus. We read that one day John was with two of his own disciples when Jesus happened to walk by. "Behold," John said to them, "there is the Lamb of God!" The two disciples left John and began to follow Jesus; one of them was the apostle Andrew, brother of Simon Peter. John was letting go of his own self-interest and pointing people to Jesus. What a wonderful model for Church leaders today! Recently Pope Francis chided the crowds for shouting "Francis! Francis! Pope Francis!" "What about Jesus?" the pope said. "I'd rather you'd cry out 'Jesus! Jesus is Lord!' All right?" This is a good lesson for all of us.

Later, when Jesus began preaching on the other side of the Jordan River, John's disciples were getting upset. They came and said to John: "Rabbi, you know the one who was with you on the other side of the Jordan? The one you authorized with your witness? Well, he's now competing with us. He's baptizing, too, and everyone's going to him instead of us" (John 3:26). (Implication: That's not right!) But with wondrous humility John replied:

> *"It's not possible for a person to succeed—I'm talking about eternal success—without heaven's help. You yourselves were there when I made it public that I was not the Messiah but simply the one sent ahead of him to get things ready. The one who gets the bride is, by definition, the bridegroom. And the bridegroom's friend, his "best man"—that's me—in place at his side where he can hear every word, is genuinely happy. How could he be jealous when he knows that the wedding is finished and the marriage is off to a good start?*
>
> *"That's why my cup is running over. This is the assigned moment for him to move into the center, while I slip off to the sidelines."*
>
> John 3:27-30

This is why I always think of John the Baptist as "a man without ego."

John speaks truth to power—as we sometimes are called to do

After Jesus had begun his own preaching and healing ministry, John turned his attention to Herod, one of Rome's Jewish puppet kings. John confronted him for his seducing and marrying his own brother's wife, Herodias. "That's wrong and you know it," John said in no uncertain terms. Herod responded by throwing him into prison. But that wasn't good enough for Herodias; she wanted John dead. Herod himself was ambivalent about John: "Herod was in awe of John. Convinced that he was a holy man, he gave him special treatment. Whenever he listened to him he was miserable with guilt—and yet he couldn't stay away. Something in John kept pulling him back" (Mark 6:19-20).

On Herod's birthday, the king put on a sumptuous banquet for his courtiers, military officers, and local politicians. At one point, when the guests had plenty to drink, the daughter of Herodias came in and performed an enticing strip-tease to the cheers of all the guests, including Herod. He called her over and said, "You were terrific! Now—ask for whatever you wish and I'll give it to you—even if it's half of my kingdom!" The girl left the room and asked her mother what she should do. Her mother said, "Ask for the head of John the Baptist!" The girl went back and told Herod. He was stunned, told her he couldn't do that, but his guests kept taunting him: "A promise is a promise. Give her what she wants!" So the king gave in. He ordered the executioner to behead John and bring the head to Herodias (see Mark 6:17-28). When Matthew tells this story in his Gospel, he adds an interesting note: "When Jesus got the news, he slipped away by boat to an out-of-the-way place by himself" (Matthew 14:13). He probably needed to grieve for the death of his cousin and friend. He must have also realized that he would soon become a marked man himself.

It is undoubtedly important for mental health that we have a good sense of self-worth. Otherwise, we will be weighed down by a nagging sense of inadequacy, inferiority, and lack of self-confidence. But the danger is we can become driven by what the brilliant psychiatrist Karen Horney called "the search for glory"—the compulsion to make a name for ourselves, to acquire more possessions, to move up in the status hierarchy, to be "Number One." If we fall short of our ambition, we can become unhappy, angry, frustrated, and feel like a failure.

This search for glory can also poison our relationships. If we have to be the center of attention, to be in control, then others better not get in our way. Think about it: How many marriages and families are in conflict because members are always competing rather than cooperating? How many problems poison the workplace because people with big egos are forever demanding their own way? Even in our churches: How many dissensions are created when one clique has to be in control or regard themselves as superior to the others? How often is the Gospel of Jesus undermined because people with big egos can't work together?

> We are to pursue our excellence in ways that do not interfere with the well-being of others.

John the Baptist is a model of one who was free from the search for glory. St. Thomas Aquinas once gave a wonderful definition for humility. True humility, he said, is "the reasonable pursuit of one's own excellence." Think about that. It means, first of all, that we have an excellence that is God-given. We are made in the divine image and are endowed with various gifts and abilities. Second, it is God's will that we pursue that excellence, that is, foster, develop, and utilize our gifts to the best of our ability. And finally, we are to pursue our excellence "reasonably," that is, in ways that do not harm our own health or interfere with the well-being of others. Pride, then, is the un-reasonable pursuit of our excellence—pretending to have abilities we do not possess or flaunting the ones we do have so as to shame or humiliate others. John the Baptist exhibited true humility in everything he did. He was no shrinking violet; that is obvious. But he knew who he was: the precursor of another. "I'm not even worthy to hold his coat for him" (John 1:27).

John struggled with doubts—as each of us will

As strong and as humble as he was, John the Baptist struggled with doubts. At one point, while he was in Herod's prison, he sent messengers to Jesus asking: "John the Baptizer sent us to ask you, 'Are you the One we've been expecting, or are we still waiting?'" (Luke 7:19). What prompted this surprising question? Like most of his contemporaries, perhaps John was expecting a more fiery Messiah, one who would thunder against the evils of his time and perhaps even call down fire from heaven, as the great Elijah had done. Instead, he hears that Jesus is preaching compassion for the poor and forgiveness for sinner; healing the blind, the lame and the sick; saying not a word about overthrowing the corrupt Roman rule over the country. Even John must have thought, "Maybe I've been wrong about my cousin; maybe he is not the promised Messiah after all."

So when John's messengers ask Jesus if he is really "the one we've been expecting," Jesus replies, first with action and only then with words.

> In the next two or three hours Jesus healed many from diseases, distress, and evil spirits. To many of the blind he gave the gift of sight. Then he gave his answer: "Go back and tell John what you have just seen and heard:
>
> The blind see,
> The lame walk,
> Lepers are cleansed,
> The deaf hear,
> The dead are raised,
> The wretched of the earth
>   have God's salvation hospitality extended to them.

"Is this what you were expecting? Then count yourselves fortunate!"

Luke 7:21-23

Jesus told John's disciples to assure John that he had not been wrong about Jesus, that this is just what Isaiah had prophesied (see Isaiah 35:3-6). John had done his work well, and Jesus blessed him for it. Imagine the great relief John felt when the messengers relayed those words to him in prison. Then Jesus paid this final tribute to John: "Let me lay it out for you as plainly as I can: No one in history surpasses John the Baptizer" (Luke 7:28).

It is helpful for us to recall this last story about John the Baptist. Sometimes we also struggle with doubts in regard to our Christian faith. Thoughts like these sometimes hang over our heads like a cloud: Does God really exist? Are those stories in the Bible really true? Was Jesus truly divine? Did he really rise from the dead? Are we destined for eternity—or is death the final act in the drama of life? These questions are not trivial. How we answer them will determine the whole course of our life and all the major decisions we have to make. We need not feel guilty or ashamed if we have doubts like these. We do not have absolute, scientific proof for the truths of our faith. If we did, we couldn't call it "faith;" we'd call it "certainty." At the same time, greater minds than ours over the centuries have examined the claims of our Christian faith and concluded that they are both reasonable and coherent. But they require us to accept some mysteries that we may not fully comprehend. It is not that different in the domain in science: the more discoveries are made, the more mysteries and uncertainties appear. As the Psalmist prayed:

> *Your thoughts—how rare, how beautiful!*
> *God, I'll never comprehend them!*
> *I couldn't even begin to count them—*
> *any more than I could count the sand of the sea.*

Psalm 139:-17-18

Our task, as was John the Baptist's, is to seek answers for our doubts as far as possible; but then to bow humbly before the mysteries that lie beyond us.

QUESTIONS FOR DISCUSSION AND REFLECTION

1. What are some aspects of John the Baptist's life and character that specially appeal to you?

2. What do you think of John's spiritual axiom: Christ must increase; I must decrease? How does it connect with your own life? Explain your answer.

3. Have you ever been called upon to speak "truth to power"? What happened?

4. Name someone you know who practices true humility. Does that person follow what St. Thomas Aquinas called "the reasonable pursuit of one's own excellence"? Describe how.

5. How do you try to deal with doubts of faith? Give some examples.

JOSEPH OF NAZARETH

Man for Our Times?

We actually have relatively little biographical information about Joseph from the Bible. We are told he worked as a carpenter, and artists usually picture him in a wood-working shop alongside the boy Jesus, turning out tables, chairs, cabinets, and the like. But recent historians suggest quite a different image. We now know that the Romans were building a new city named Sephhoris about a mile or two from Nazareth. Most likely, Joseph and Jesus were construction workers rather than cabinet makers. They would walk each day to Sephhoris to hew and erect the wooden beams for the new buildings; it was hard manual work, requiring heavy lifting and careful fitting of the beams. Indeed, computer enhancement of the famous Shroud of Turin, believed to be the burial cloth for the body of Jesus, reveals a very muscular young man. Very likely, Joseph had also been shaped and toughened by hard manual labor.

We first meet Joseph in the Gospel of Matthew. He is engaged to be married to young Mary of Nazareth, who suddenly and out of the blue tells him she has just become pregnant by the mysterious power of the Holy Spirit. Joseph loves Mary deeply and wants to believe her, but naturally he has doubts. What man wouldn't? Joseph must have thought: This can't be true! What if she has just imagined this? Or she has really slept with another man and is too ashamed to admit it?

The Bible notes: "Before they came to the marriage bed, Joseph discovered she was pregnant. (It was by the Holy Spirit, but he didn't know that.) Joseph, chagrined but noble, determined to take care of things quietly so Mary would not be disgraced" (Matthew 1:19).

Joseph is a just man, meaning that he wants to obey the Law of Moses. According to that Law, engagement was just as binding as marriage, though sexual relations were not allowed. If one partner was unfaithful during the engagement period, the other was required to obtain a divorce. But Joseph had two options: either a public trial or a private decision. He took the whole matter to prayer, and opted for the second choice. If Mary has indeed been unfaithful, Joseph is being obedient to the Law. But if she truly is pregnant by the power of God, then she doesn't need Joseph; she belongs to God, and God will provide for her.

But as a man, imagine Joseph's feelings. His heart is broken. He has to give up the woman he truly loves. Moreover, he has been either betrayed or replaced, but he is definitely not needed. As someone once said, "Even if you lose to God in a love triangle, it still hurts!"

God intervenes in Joseph's life— as God does in ours

But then God intervenes. Joseph (his namesake in the Old Testament was a dreamer as well) has a wonderful dream. An angel of God appears to him and says:

> *"Joseph, son of David, don't hesitate to get married. Mary's pregnancy is Spirit-conceived. God's Holy Spirit has made her pregnant. She will bring a son to birth, and when she does, you, Joseph, will name him Jesus—'God saves'—because he will save his people from their sins."*
> *Matthew 1:20-21*

Matthew adds:

This would bring the prophet's embryonic sermon to full term:

Watch for this—a virgin will get pregnant and bear a son;
They will name him Immanuel
(Hebrew for "God is with us").

Matthew 1:22-23

Joseph's painful dilemma is resolved in a wondrous way. God tells him: "Joseph, you still have an important place in my plan and in the life of Mary and her child. You are to name him (which was the father's right in Jewish law), and you are to love and care for this family—I entrust them to you. Go ahead and do what your heart wants to do!" Matthew's account concludes, "Then Joseph woke up. He did exactly what God's angel commanded in the dream: He married Mary" (Matthew 1:24).

This story reveals how human Joseph was: he was hurt; he had doubts; he didn't know what he should do. He really loved Mary and was willing to risk the gossip that would surely take place when she gave birth so soon after their marriage. But Joseph was committed to doing the right thing, not what was the easiest or face-saving thing for himself.

One of the key lessons to learn from Joseph is that he was willing to slow down in the midst of a crisis and seek guidance in prayer. It is a marvelous image that Joseph "woke up" and then "did exactly what God's angel commanded." In other words, he made his decision in the light of God's will, which is always to act with love. This is a fine example for us when we are faced with difficult decisions, especially those that will affect people who are close to us.

A question often arises here, especially from our Protestant friends: Did Mary and Joseph have other children besides Jesus? The Catholic Church maintains the faith of the early Church in teaching that Jesus was the only child of Mary and that she remained a virgin all her life. Several problems arise in connection with that teaching. First there is Matthew's statement that Joseph "did not consummate the marriage until she had the baby" (Matthew 1:25). Some point to the use of the English word *until* in the New American Bible, the Douay-Rheims, and The Message translations as indicating that the couple did, in fact, have relations *after* the birth of Jesus. This is a perfectly logical conclusion and what we would expect to have happened in real life. However, both the Hebrew and Greek words for *until* imply nothing about the future; they simply state what did not happen up to the time of the event mentioned (in this case, the birth of Jesus). Another text says that one day while Jesus was teaching the crowds "his mother and brothers" showed up, wishing to speak with him (see Matthew 12:46-47). But the Hebrew language is also short on nouns, and we know that the same words for brother and sister are also used for nieces, nephews, and cousins. So these texts cannot be used to prove that Mary and Joseph had other children.

But this is the wrong way to think about biblical stories. They are filled with miraculous events that are meant to teach us a lesson. In this case, the lesson is in the implication: Mary and Joseph lived in a chaste marriage. Therefore (thinking only of Joseph here), he had to deal with sexual desires, including for other women. It is good for all of us men to remember this, including those who are in great marriages, but especially those who are single, divorced, widowed, vowed to celibacy, or in a marriage where sexual relations are not a regular event for whatever reason. Joseph is a good role model for us, as well as a strong intercessor to help us maintain chastity in whatever sexual situation we find ourselves.

Joseph becomes a father—as we all must do one way or another

I once read a short play that made the Christmas story come alive for me in a dramatic way. Joseph tells Mary he thinks he can add on to their house to make room for the child; he also shows her plans for "a cradle that rocks." Mary exclaims what a happy time it was as the day for the child's birth was drawing near. But then

Joseph's face turns dark with a frown. "Mary," he says, "the Romans have decreed a census. There are no exceptions—we have to go to Bethlehem because that is the town of David, our ancestral home."

At this point in the play, Mary tells the audience how she cried for days, thinking of the long trip when she is close to delivery time. "Riding the donkey was almost as uncomfortable as walking," she tells us. As they near Bethlehem, she informs Joseph the contractions are starting. "Okay," he says, "I'll find us a place."

"It wasn't much," Mary explains, "just a cattle shelter. But at least it was dry and out of the wind. And it smelled of animals and hay. There was no cradle like the one that Joseph had made—just a cow's manger to lay the baby."

"I felt awful," Mary continues, "but thinking back, I learned something important that night: God says, 'My ways are not your ways.' We had prepared a nice room for this child, but he chose a manger, as if he thought of himself as food. He didn't belong just to us, but to everyone. So keep this in mind: Jesus shows up when and where you least expect him."

Mary's thoughts and words in the play were a great comfort to Joseph, who probably had been tempted to blame himself for not preparing better for the birth of his son. How many fathers feel inadequate, especially with their firstborn child? And how many of us who are not biological fathers feel inadequate as we try to generate life in other ways? Here is another story of how Joseph may have had these same feelings.

Recall again that Mary and Joseph are faithful Jews, obedient to the Law of Moses. So after forty days they come to the Temple in Jerusalem to present their child for consecration to the Lord, as the Jewish Law required. This gives Luke, the evangelist, the occasion to have us reflect on the coming of the Messiah in fulfillment of the Old Testament prophecies.

Luke draws our attention to two special elders, Simeon and Anna. They represent what is sometimes called "the faithful remnant" of Israel: Jews who had not abandoned their faith in God, as so many others had done after the Roman conquest of Palestine. These two minor characters continued to pray, observe the religious practices, and hope for the restoration of God's reign in Israel. Luke says Simeon was "a good man, a man who lived in the prayerful expectancy of help for Israel. And the Holy Spirit was on him" (Luke 2:25). Simeon had been told by the Holy Spirit that he would not die before seeing the Messiah. So when Mary and Joseph brought their child into the Temple, Simeon rushed over, took the child in his arms, and praised God.

> "God, you can now release your servant;
>   release me in peace as you promised.
> With my own eyes I've seen your salvation;
>   it's now out in the open for everyone to see:
> A God-revealing light to the non-Jewish nations,
>   and of glory for your people Israel."
>
> *Luke 2:29-32*

Next came Anna, a devout 84-year-old who never left the Temple, but worshiped night and day with fasting and prayer. "At the very time Simeon was praying, she showed up, broke into an anthem of praise to God, and talked about the child to all who were waiting expectantly for the freeing of Jerusalem" (Luke 2:38).

We always focus on Mary in this story, but think of what it must have meant to Joseph after all he had been through. It must have been a source of great joy and encouragement to Joseph to have his son recognized by these two holy people. But there is also a note of sadness and foreboding. After praising God, Simeon turned to Mary and said:

> "This child marks both the failure and
>   the recovery of many in Israel,
> A figure misunderstood and contradicted—
>   the pain of a sword-thrust through you—
> But the rejection will force honesty,
>   as God reveals who they really are."
>
> *Luke 2:34-35*

Simeon was saying that when the time comes people will take sides—for or against their child. As a result their own hearts will be broken with sorrow. Like the Old Testament prophets, Jesus would have to face opposition and rejection. His life would include suffering and tragedy as well as enthusiasm and final victory. Listening to this dire prophecy, as a man and a husband Joseph must have wondered: How can I prevent Mary's suffering—or at least help her through it? Yet, according to tradition, Joseph died before Jesus began his public life. He must have felt in some way that he had failed his wife and son.

One of the sharp pains of fatherhood comes with not being able to provide for one's family. This was surely the case with Joseph at the time of the birth of Jesus. More generally, many males (myself certainly included) have a seemingly innate tendency to want to "fix" whatever (or whoever) is troubled. This is certainly a good thing. It can lead us to take initiative in planning for contingencies and doing preventive maintenance. But it can also become an obsession or a compulsion, driving us to rush in where we may not be wanted or blaming ourselves for whatever goes wrong.

One of the sharp pains of fatherhood comes with not being able to provide well for one's family.

Sometimes things simply go wrong for no reason, or at least they are not our fault. We may be laid off from work, suffer an accident, make a wrong investment, or say the wrong thing at a critical time. It is unhelpful to waste energy on endless regrets. We need to forgive ourselves and move on. Most of the time, we can honestly say, "I did the best I could with the knowledge I had at the time." If we cannot say that, we simply apologize and resolve to be more thoughtful next time.

Another reality Joseph had to face as a man, a husband, and a father: We men cannot always protect our loved ones from harm or pain. One of our deepest fears is feeling helpless in the face of the suffering of those we love. Sometimes our only recourse is to be at their side, praying and offering our loving support. We will see this theme recur in the next two phases of Joseph's life.

Joseph has to flee danger—as we sometimes must

One of the events that takes place after the birth of Jesus is the visit of the magi (scholars, astrologers?) from the East. Their sighting of an unusually bright star signaled to them the birth of a new king. The story is described in detail in Matthew's Gospel (see 2:1-15). When King Herod heard the magi's story, he felt threatened: would this new king displace him? In his paranoia, he planned a pre-emptive strike: kill off all the newborn babies in and around Bethlehem, much as the king of Egypt had done with the Hebrew children at the time of Moses.

But once again, God intervened to save a child, just as he had with Moses. We read: "God's angel showed up again in Joseph's dream and commanded, 'Get up. Take the child and his mother and flee to Egypt. Stay until further notice. Herod is on the hunt for this child, and wants to kill him'" (Matthew 2:13).

Once again, Joseph had to make an untimely journey, this time for a much greater distance. This reminds me of the many men I have known who have had to move their families several times for a variety of reasons. There's a bit of holy irony in this move, however. The land that once enslaved the Hebrew people and Moses now becomes a refuge for the new Moses, Jesus of Nazareth. Egypt was a safer place at that point in history: Herod had no power there because Egypt had been under Roman control since 30 B.C. Very likely Matthew had in mind another connection. In the Old Testament Joseph brought his father Jacob (also called Israel) to Egypt to save him from famine. Now in the New Testament, a new Joseph brings the new Israel (Jesus) to Egypt for safety.

But again, think of all the questions Joseph had to face as the husband and father: How long will we be there? What should we take along? Where will we live? Will I be able to find work?

Most likely the Holy Family was able to find a home and work among the other Jewish settlers there. We do not know how long they remained in Egypt, but it was probably not much more than a year. Matthew says that after the death of Herod, an angel again appeared to Joseph with the message that he should return. The family then settled again in Nazareth. Still, this must have been a very stressful event for Joseph to be compelled to drag his family to a strange country and back "with only the clothes on their backs," as the saying goes. It was certainly not a great career path for him. Truly, Joseph and his wife and son had become refugees.

At this point, the Gospel of Luke adds: "There the child grew strong in body and wise in spirit. And the grace of God was on him" (Luke 2:40). At this point, it seems that Joseph's role became like that of other fathers of small children. He provided for Jesus, played with him, taught him the Aramaic language (a dialect of Hebrew), upheld the family rules, helped him explore the world of nature, and so on. Most importantly, it was the Jewish father's duty to provide religious formation. So Joseph taught Jesus his Scripture and prayers, Jewish history, and the observance of the Sabbath and yearly Jewish feasts. He also took Jesus to the synagogue service every Sabbath day. Luke notes that when Jesus began his public ministry as an adult, "As he always did on the Sabbath, he went to the meeting place" (Luke 4:16). I always like to use this passage to remind people: "If weekly worship was important to Jesus, it certainly ought to be at least as important for us." And it was Jesus' father who taught him this.

Joseph's last appearance—another failure that turned into a victory

The Bible recounts only one other event in the life of Joseph. Because he and Mary were devout Jews, they made a regular pilgrimage to Jerusalem for the holy feast of Passover. This is pretty amazing to those of us who are used to jumping in a car to get someplace. Nazareth is about 60 miles from Jerusalem, and they only way to get there at the time was to walk. But they did it every year!

One particular year, the child Jesus accompanied them. The rabbis taught that a boy reaches manhood on his thirteenth birthday; but if he could understand the meaning of God's commandments, he could be bound by them before he reached thirteen. The Bible says Jesus made this pilgrimage when he was twelve, so it shows that he was a little ahead of the average Jewish boy in his religious understanding. Joseph was obviously doing a good job of religious education.

The Passover feast lasted eight days, but the pilgrims were required to stay for only the first two; so people would leave the festivities at different times and days. We are told only this: "When it was over and they left for home, the child Jesus stayed behind in Jerusalem, but his parents didn't know it" (Luke 2:43). This could happen quite easily, as any parent will tell you. Mary and Joseph presumed Jesus was with his cousins and friends on the return journey. Remember, the people from Nazareth were probably all walking together in a large group, and the kids were probably running ahead or dragging behind as they always do.

When Joseph and Mary realized Jesus was not with the group, they were stunned. Again, we can only imagine their feelings—probably a mixture of fear and guilt. "Why weren't we more careful? One of us should have made sure he was in the caravan." Perhaps they even said some unpleasant things to each other. They hustled back to Jerusalem, which to them would have been "the big city."

"The next day they found him in the Temple seated among the teachers, listening to them, and asking questions" (Luke 2:46), the Bible says simply and kind of matter-of-factly. This is after three days: one day to leave the city, another day to return, and a third day for the search. This was not just a simple case of losing track of a child. Jesus was lost.

And what did they find him doing? Sitting in the midst of the teachers (rabbis) in the temple, listening and asking questions. Luke says: "The teachers were all quite taken with him, impressed with the sharpness of his answers. But his parents were not impressed; they were upset and hurt" (Luke 2:47-48).

Mary rebukes Jesus in no uncertain terms: "Young man, why have you done this to us? Your father and I have been half out of our minds looking for you" (Luke 2:48). How many parents have said things like this to children who have stayed out beyond their 12-year-olds' curfew, much less disappearing for three days?

Jesus' reply shows little empathy for their anxiety: "Why were you looking for me? Didn't you know that I had to be here, dealing with the things of my Father?" (Luke 2:49). Scholars say his harsh reply is less a rebuke than an attempt to instruct them. As Raymond Brown says, "His presence in the Temple and talking with the teachers is indicative of where his true vocation lies: in the service of God who is his Father, not at the beck and call of his natural family."

This might be a good time to address Jesus' image of God as "Abba," which means "Father" or, even more familiarly, "Daddy." It must have struck Joseph as odd to hear his son talk about God as "Father." Did this mean that Jesus was unsatisfied or disrespectful of Joseph? I think just the opposite. The very fact that Jesus would use this name to capture the image of the loving God he knew intimately shows me more than anything else how much Jesus loved and respected Joseph.

Still, Luke notes that "they had no idea what he was talking about" (Luke 2:50). Here again, we see the humanness of Mary and Joseph. They were often puzzled and confused about how to understand and deal with Jesus—just as so many parents with children are nowadays.

But at the end, we read that Jesus "went back to Nazareth with them, and lived obediently with them" (Luke 2:51). Again, we see that Jesus is the New Israel, the faithful one. His first loyalty and obedience is to God his Father; but he also keeps God's command to honor and obey his earthly father and mother. Joseph's role now becomes that of mentoring the teenage Jesus into adulthood: to teach him about sexuality, about the proper treatment of women, and about becoming a responsible worker.

You may have noted that I put a question mark at the end of the title for this chapter. My reason: Some may question whether Joseph can be viewed seriously as "a man for our times." After all, his person and role are unique: married to a woman who is pregnant with a miraculously conceived child; living with her in a chaste marriage; guided by God through dreams; foster-father of the Son of God. Still, we need to think more carefully about the commonalities of Joseph's experience as a man and our own. First, recall how often Joseph's plans were interrupted and dramatically changed: the unexpected trip to Bethlehem at the very time Mary's baby was due; the fear-inspired exodus into Egypt because of Herod's murderous intent; the anxiety over losing his son in Jerusalem. Are these not the kinds of things you experience as a male?

How often have your plans and dreams been interrupted and radically changed by a job transfer involving a move to a strange location; an unanticipated pregnancy; an extended job layoff or a cut in salary; an illness or accident requiring a long recuperation or even living with a life-long handicap; having to change plans in order to care for aging parents or in-laws or even your spouse? At times like these, like Joseph, we often find ourselves questioning the ways of God: Why is this happening? What are you asking of me? Whose fault is it—or is it just bad luck? We need not be ashamed of these responses to stress: they are normal and natural. Our call or vocation as men is to surrender to God's will in trust; to recall God's oft-repeated promise in the Bible: "Do not be afraid, for I am with you." That was the truth Joseph had to cling to while coping with the unforeseen twists in his own life. And sometimes, looking back, we are able to see the grace and blessing that were present in those troubled times. We be-

> Our call or vocation as men is to surrender to God's will in trust.

came more humble, more compassionate with the sufferings of others, grew closer to our loved ones, and became more reliant on God than on ourselves. Other times, we just have to trust that things will somehow work out, even if we never understand them.

Another connection we have with Joseph is that, in Jewish tradition, it was the father's task to provide for the children's religious formation. In contemporary society, because of the father's preoccupation with work, this task generally falls to the mother. But this should not absolve the father of all responsibility. A body of research has shown that when the father is at least somewhat involved in the children's spiritual formation, there is a marked positive effect on the children's growth and perseverance in their faith.

I was pleased when a newspaper reported on Barack Obama's commencement address to the graduates of Morehouse College, an all-black, all-male school in Atlanta. He reminded the young men that the goal of their education was to produce "good men, strong men, upright men who will better themselves so they could help others do the same."

"It betrays a poverty of ambition," the President said, "if all you think about is what goods you can buy instead of what good you can do."

Then, speaking for himself, he added, "I want to be a better father, a better husband, a better man."

Those are worthy goals for all of us men. And I believe St. Joseph would heartily agree.

A final note: In the Catholic Church calendar there are two feasts in honor of St. Joseph. The first is "The Solemnity of St. Joseph" on March 19, recalling his role as husband of Mary and foster-father of Jesus. This is an ancient feast dating back to the tenth century. The other is "St. Joseph the Worker," celebrated on May 1. This began in the 1950s as a response to the Communist observance of May Day paying tribute to "workers of the world" usually displaying power in a huge parade of Soviet soldiers and military weapons. The May feast honoring Joseph was intended to remind *all* workers of their dignity as participants in God's continuing work of creation by the wise use of their knowledge and skills. St. Joseph is also often invoked as a special intercessor at the time of death. Tradition holds that he died in the presence of both Jesus and Mary. This is why he is honored as "patron saint of a happy death."

QUESTIONS FOR REFLECTION AND DISCUSSION

1. How do you deal with those times when you don't understand the ways of God? Give an example.

2. Reflect on one of the moves/changes you have had to make. What was especially difficult about it? How did it affect your loved ones? Where did you find the grace/blessing to deal with it?

3. In what ways are you trying to become a better husband, a better father, a better man? Make a list and post it someplace where you can review it each morning.

4. Have you ever had to flee a situation? How did it make you feel?

5. What does obedience mean to you? When have you been obedient to others? When have you demanded others to be obedient to you? What did these experiences have in common?

PETER

More Heart Than Rock

I find that for most Christian men, Peter is their favorite biblical figure after Jesus. When I ask them why, the answer is usually some variation of "because he's so much like me." We know a good deal about Peter. He is mentioned almost 200 times in the New Testament, more than the other eleven apostles combined.

We encounter Peter in the very first chapter of the Gospel of John. John the Baptist pointed Jesus out to two of his own disciples, calling him "God's Passover Lamb." One of the disciples was Andrew, the brother of Simon Peter. When Andrew introduced his brother to Jesus, "Jesus took one look up and said, 'You're John's son, Simon? From now on your name is Cephas' (or Peter, which means 'Rock')" (John 1:42). By changing his name on their very first encounter, Jesus was telling Simon he saw something special in him. Did "rock" imply being hard-headed or stubborn? Very likely, given the stories we are about to hear. But later, we will see that Jesus established his Church on someone rock-solid. So, we might even say that Jesus enjoyed a good pun with the rest of us!

Peter learns about Jesus the hard way— as most of us do

Next we find Jesus coming to Peter's house in the town of Capernaum and healing his mother-in-law of a severe fever. It appears that he made Peter's house kind of a home base where he could return after preaching in the surrounding towns and countryside. We will avoid all mother-in-law jokes here, men.

One of Peters' life-changing moments occurred when he was cleaning his fishing nets. Jesus abruptly asked Peter to row him out a short distance from land so he could teach the people from the boat. Peter agreed readily. But then Jesus told (not asked) him to row out into the deep water and lower his nets for a catch of fish. We can just imagine Peter's thoughts: "What does this rabbi (or whatever he is) know about fishing? No one fishes in broad daylight here; the fish dive to the bottom and rest there till evening; that's when we catch them."

But after making some objection, as most of us would if some relative stranger told us how to run our business, Peter complies with Jesus' request. Who knows why? Maybe he just wanted to teach Jesus a lesson in humility. All of a sudden, though, he and his companions find their nets filled with fish, enough to fill two boats almost to the sinking point. Peter goes down on his knees (we presume he was back on shore by then) and says, "Master, leave. I'm a sinner and can't handle this holiness. Leave me to myself" (Luke 5: 8).

Note that, in response to Peter's statement, Jesus does not deny that Peter is a sinner, but he calls him anyway—as he calls us—to quit being afraid, let go of the past, and become an active disciple, helping Jesus in his mission of bringing all people back to God: "There is nothing to fear. From now on you'll be fishing for men and women" (Luke 5:10).

Another time, Peter is once again on the Sea of Galilee. This is after he has just seen Jesus feed 5,000 hungry people with five loaves of bread and a few fish—a miraculous event. Jesus tells the disciples to cross the lake while he stays behind to pray. About half-way across, they encounter one of the sudden storms for which that large lake is famous. The wind and waves toss the boat around like a toy. Suddenly they see Jesus coming toward them, walking on the water. They are terrified, thinking it is a ghost. But Jesus tells them, "Courage, it's me. Don't be afraid" (Matthew

14:26). Notice how often Jesus tells us to let go of our fear. He does the same after he rises from the dead. He is not telling us, "Don't be afraid of the ghost." He is telling us, "You have nothing to fear if I am with you."

Typically, the impetuous Peter says, "Master, if it's really you, call me to come to you on the water" (Matthew 14:28). Notice that even here, Peter is testing whether Jesus is who he says he is. Jesus invites him to come, and Peter starts walking on the water. Haven't we all had the feeling that we could do anything if we just put our minds to it? But when he sees the waves and feels the powerful wind, Peter becomes frightened and starts to sink. "Master, save me!" he cries (Matthew 14:30). We've all been *there* too, haven't we? Jesus stretches out his hand and brings them both into the boat. The wind suddenly dies down and everything becomes calm. Jesus, kindly and with humor, rebukes Peter: "Faint-heart, what got into you?" (Matthew 14:30). Peter and the rest of the disciples simply say, "This is it! You are God's Son for sure!" (Matthew 14:33).

The moment of conversion comes when we find we need spiritual resources and simply don't have them.

Reflecting on the call of Peter to be a disciple, it would be good for us to ask ourselves: "How am I led to want to be more than a Sunday-only Christian?" Perhaps your answer will come through the example of your wife or a best friend. Or when your children begin asking questions about the Bible or church or why bad things happen to good people. Or when you yourself are hit with a crisis or serious problem and your usual coping strategies didn't work.

The moment of conversion (or "turning around") comes when we find we need spiritual resources and simply don't have them. Somehow, we begin looking more closely at Jesus and saying to ourselves: "There is something so attractive about this man—his teachings, the way he treats people—that I want to follow him, learn from him, maybe even help him carry out his mission." As with Peter, fishing isn't enough anymore. We want something more out of life than having the most toys when we die.

I once came across a book by a psychologist, Richard Miller. It was not, in my opinion, a great book; but it had a wonderful title: *How to Want What You Have*. Most self-help books nowadays talk about "How to get what you want." This one is about wanting what you *already have*. Too many of us are driven, Miller says, by wanting MORE (always capitalized). But, despite acquiring more and more, we are never satisfied. So what if we could turn our emotional energy toward appreciating and being grateful for what we already have? Perhaps we would become free of the compulsion to acquire MORE and begin to enjoy, take pleasure in, share with loved ones and others what we already possess: not only material things, but spiritual gifts and blessings. Think, for example, of the beauties of nature, of music, of friendships, of good books or movies, or of walks or drives on country paths or roads.

Peter gives it up for Jesus—as we are called to do

Jesus had been slowly forming his disciples into new ways of thinking about God and how God's people ought to be living. One day he pulled them aside and said, "What are people saying about who the Son of Man is?" (Matthew 16:13). This is one of the only indications in the Gospels that Jesus cared what people thought of him. In fact, of course, it was his disciples—including us—whose opinion mattered to him.

The disciples were like a bunch of school children, trying to guess the right answer: "Some think he is John the Baptizer, some say Elijah, some Jeremiah or one of the other prophets" (Matthew 16:14).

Like any good teacher, Jesus finally had to be explicit about what he was asking: "And how about you? Who do you say I am?" (Matthew 16:15).

Here is where Peter rose to the occasion and gave the correct answer: "You're the Christ, the Messiah, the Son of the living God" (Matthew 16:16). This is the statement of faith all Christians have to make—not just once in our lives but every single day.

This reply clearly pleased Jesus. He turned to Peter and said:

"God bless you, Simon, son of Jonah! You didn't get that answer out of books or from teachers. My Father in heaven, God himself, let you in on this secret of who I really am. And now I'm going to tell you who you are, really are. You are Peter, a rock. This is the rock on which I will put together my church, a church so expansive with energy that not even the gates of hell will be able to keep it out.

"And that's not all. You will have complete and free access to God's kingdom, keys to open any and every door: no more barriers between heaven and earth, earth and heaven. A yes on earth is yes in heaven. A no on earth is no in heaven."
Matthew 16:17-19

Keys in the Bible are always symbols of authority (see Isaiah 22:22; Revelation 3:7). Catholics believe it is right here that Jesus himself made Peter the head of the apostles and by extension his successors (the popes) the head of the entire Church. We call this "the ministry of leadership," and it is not about power at all but rather about service. We further believe that Jesus implicitly promised that he will guide the Church so that it will not teach error about the basic Christian message in any substantive way until the end of time.

Immediately following this important moment, a surprising thing happened—one of the strangest encounters in all of Scripture.

Then Jesus made it clear to his disciples that it was now necessary for him to go to Jerusalem, submit to an ordeal of suffering at the hands of the religious leaders, be killed, and then on the third day be raised up alive. Peter took him in hand, protesting, "Impossible, Master! That can never be!"

But Jesus didn't swerve. "Peter, get out of my way. Satan, get lost. You have no idea how God works."

Then Jesus went to work on his disciples. "Anyone who intends to come with me has to let me lead. You're not in the driver's seat; I am. Don't run from suffering; embrace it. Follow me and I'll show you how. Self-help is no help at all. Self-sacrifice is the way, my way, to finding yourself, your true self. What kind of deal is it to get everything you want but lose yourself? What could you ever trade your soul for?

"Don't be in such a hurry to go into business for yourself. Before you know it the Son of Man will arrive with all the splendor of his Father, accompanied by an army of angels. You'll get everything you have coming to you, a personal gift. This isn't pie in the sky by and by. Some of you standing here are going to see it take place, see the Son of Man in kingdom glory."

Matthew 16:21-28

How's that for spinning someone's head on a swivel? Right after giving him the "keys to the kingdom," Jesus calls Peter "Satan!" Peter and the others were left to ponder this message for whatever it might mean. The shadow of the cross had just passed over them. We need to recall that the notion of a suffering Messiah was completely foreign and even abhorrent to the disciples. As we saw with John the Baptist, the common expectation was that the Messiah would be a conquering hero who would drive the Romans out of the country and restore Israel to its former glory. Suffering and the cross had no place in this scenario. So Jesus had to make it plain that his redeeming mission must include suffering and death. It took a lot longer for Peter to understand this.

Peter learns about servant leadership—
and so should we

From now on the Gospels say little about Peter until the time nears for the death of Jesus. The scene is the so-called "Last Supper," the night before Jesus dies. Jesus is seated at table with his disciples. Suddenly he gets up, puts on an apron, and begins to wash their feet. They are stunned. This is the task of slaves, not the master. Peter tries to reason with Jesus.

> *When he got to Simon Peter, Peter said, "Master, you wash my feet?"*
>
> *Jesus answered, "You don't understand now what I'm doing, but it will be clear enough to you later."*
>
> *Peter persisted, "You're not going to wash my feet—ever!"*
>
> *Jesus said, "If I don't wash you, you can't be part of what I'm doing."*
>
> *"Master!" said Peter. "Not only my feet, then. Wash my hands! Wash my head!"*
>
> *Jesus said, "If you've had a bath in the morning, you only need your feet washed now and you're clean from head to toe. My concern, you understand, is holiness, not hygiene. So now you're clean. But not every one of you." (He knew who was betraying him. That's why he said, "Not every one of you.") After he had finished washing their feet, he took his robe, put it back on, and went back to his place at the table.*
>
> *Then he said, "Do you understand what I have done to you? You address me as 'Teacher' and 'Master,' and rightly so. That is what I am. So if I, the Master and Teacher, washed your feet, you must now wash each other's feet. I've laid down a pattern for you. What I've done, you do. I'm only pointing out the obvious. A servant is not ranked above his master; an employee doesn't give orders to the employer. If you understand what I'm telling you, act like it—and live a blessed life.*
>
> John 13:6-17

Once again, Peter is the foil for Jesus' teaching. It is almost as if Jesus thought, "If I can get Peter to understand what I am trying to accomplish *anyone* should be able to."

Over the centuries many Church leaders have lost Jesus' vision of ministry. Too often they have seen themselves as lords and masters rather than servants, using their authority to stifle others rather than to help and empower them. The Second Vatican Council revived the image of servant leadership, and Pope Francis provided an inspiring example of this when, on Holy Thursday night, he celebrated Mass in a prison for juvenile offenders and humbly washed their feet.

Our natural tendency as humans is to want to be served rather than to serve. Even in the secular and business world this concept has been taking hold, beginning with Robert Greenleaf's 1977 book *Servant Leadership* (adapted for church ministry by Owen Phelps in *Leading Like Jesus*). This kind of leadership focuses on ways of fostering cooperation among work associates rather than mere compliance. It also stresses "empowerment"—encouraging employees to be creative in their work in order to better achieve the purposes of the organization. Research has shown that the best-performing organizations are those that are able to harness their people's desire to use their talents to achieve goals they believe are worthwhile.

Peter denies Jesus—which we all sometimes do

The other three Gospels, in relating the Last Supper scene, include another embarrassing account in regard to Peter. Here is Luke's rendition of the story. Jesus suddenly says to Peter:

> *"Simon, stay on your toes. Satan has tried his best to separate all of you from me, like chaff from wheat. Simon, I've prayed for you in particular that you not give in or give out. When you have come through the time of testing, turn to your companions and give them a fresh start."*
>
> *Peter said, "Master, I'm ready for anything with you. I'd go to jail for you. I'd die for you!"*

Jesus said, "I'm sorry to have to tell you this, Peter, but before the rooster crows you will have three times denied that you know me."

Luke 22:31-34

And so it happened. To his credit, when the other disciples ran away at the arrest of Jesus, Peter followed him into the courtyard of the high priest where he was going to be tried. But when some woman asked him if he was a follower of Jesus, he denied it. Later, two others raised the same question, but each time Peter denied even knowing him. "At that very moment, the last word hardly off his lips, a rooster crowed. Just then, the Master turned and looked at Peter. Peter remembered what the Master had said to him: 'Before the rooster crows, you will deny me three times.' He went out and cried and cried and cried" (Luke 22:60-62).

We can all draw hope from Peter's failure and subsequent recovery. Who among us has never slipped and fallen morally? Like Peter, we can become overconfident in our ability to follow Christ and then fall into a humiliating betrayal. I'm so glad Luke included that Jesus "turned and looked at Peter." I imagine that look as one of disappointment, but even more, one of forgiveness and love. We read next that Peter "went out and cried and cried and cried." But, unlike Judas, he did not despair. He trusted that look of love from Jesus, he repented in his heart and clung to his faith and hope in his Lord.

Peter is rehabilitated—as we will be

Finally, we must reflect on the scene that is sometimes called "the rehabilitation of Peter." It occurs only in the Gospel of John and takes place after the resurrection. Jesus had told the disciples to leave Jerusalem and go back to Galilee, where he would meet them later. They did this, but when he did not appear right away, they grew impatient. Finally, Peter said, "I'm going fishing." The others said they would join him. It's like Peter was saying, "I really don't know what's going on here. I know fishing—I'll go back to that." Doesn't this sound like us when we're not sure what we're supposed to do? Go back to what's familiar?

But after trying all night and catching nothing, at dawn they look toward shore and see a man standing there who says, "Cast your net over to the right side of the boat." When they did so, they snared a huge net full of fish. One disciple (probably John) said, "It's the Lord!" The impetuous Peter jumped into the water and waded to shore while the others hauled in the net filled with fish. Jesus had built a charcoal fire and began making breakfast for them with the fish and some bread. This is such a human scene— some friends sharing food around a campfire. Then Jesus pulls his friend (who had just denied him) aside for a private "come to Jesus" moment:

After breakfast, Jesus said to Simon Peter, "Simon, son of John, do you love me more than these?"

"Yes, Master, you know I love you."

Jesus said, "Feed my lambs."

He then asked a second time, "Simon, son of John, do you love me?"

"Yes, Master, you know I love you."

Jesus said, "Shepherd my sheep."

Then he said it a third time: "Simon, son of John, do you love me?"

Peter was upset that he asked for the third time, "Do you love me?" so he answered, "Master, you know everything there is to know. You've got to know that I love you."

Jesus said, "Feed my sheep. I'm telling you the very truth now: When you were young you dressed yourself and went wher- ever you wished, but when you get old you'll have to stretch out your hands while someone else dresses you and takes you where you don't want to go." He said this to hint at the kind of

*death by which Peter would glorify God. And then he com-
manded, "Follow me."*

John 21:15-19

Note that Peter dared not make any comparisons with the
others, as he had done at the Last Supper ("Even if they should
all leave you, I will not!"). Two more times Jesus asked the same
question, and Peter gave the same answer: "You know I love you."
A simple, straightforward statement of faith. It's as if Peter needed
to atone for his triple denial of Jesus in the courtyard, and now
he knew that he was completely forgiven. But Jesus had one more
message for him. He foretold where Peter's love for Jesus would
lead him—to his own cross.

When I read that passage, I can't help thinking of the day
when I may be "led away" to a nursing home or the equivalent.
I hope I will have the grace to trust that
rock-bottom promise of my Lord and
Savior: "Do not be afraid. I will never for-
sake you or abandon you."

If not from the Church, then where will we draw moral and spiritual guidance?

As we have seen, Peter's profession of
faith and Jesus' promise that the powers
of hell will not finally prevail against his
Church is a key moment in the Gospels.
Catholics believe that the Church has a
hierarchical structure that is needed to
insure that the teachings of Jesus will be handed on without dis-
tortion or substantive error. Otherwise, any individual or group
would be free to interpret the Scriptures in their own private way
and without any accountability. We see plenty of that today.

But people today often find difficulty with Church authority.
They want the freedom to think and decide for themselves what to
believe, without having to subscribe to creeds or doctrines. They
say, "No church should tell me how to live my life." But consider
that statement: If not from the Church, then where will we draw
moral and spiritual guidance? From talk radio hosts and their

guests? From opinion polls? From reading the latest popular author or movie? Most of us would be hesitant to trust those sources.

What is left? My own experience, my own feelings, my own conscience? That concept has a strong appeal because it resonates so well with the spirit of American individualism. But is private conscience really always an adequate guide? What if my conscience tells me I should honor the agreement I made with you, but your conscience tells you that you are free to break it? Or, if I am living with a dull spouse, what if my conscience tells me I can liven up my life by starting an affair with someone else, even your spouse? The daily news is filled with stories of good people caught in acts of wrongdoing they had somehow rationalized as "okay in these circumstances." So maybe it's not such a bad idea to look to the Church, which has learned much from centuries of experience and reflection on human behavior for doctrinal and moral direction. That is why Peter is so important. Jesus promised him that he (and, by extension, his successors) would have the guidance of the Holy Spirit. What more could we ask for?

Peter becomes a leader—as we can if we try

The story of Peter continues in Luke's other volume, the Acts of the Apostles. We don't have room to go into all the stories involving Peter, but here are a couple of them.

Very soon after Jesus ascends into heaven, Peter emerges as leader of the community of disciples. As they are assembled, he notes that the place of Judas has to be filled in order to maintain the number of apostles at twelve, in continuity with the Old Testament twelve tribes of Israel.

> Friends, long ago the Holy Spirit spoke through David regarding Judas, who became the guide to those who arrested Jesus. That Scripture had to be fulfilled, and now has been. Judas was one of us and had his assigned place in this ministry.
>
> As you know, he took the evil bribe money and bought a small

farm. There he came to a bad end, rupturing his belly and spilling his guts. Everybody in Jerusalem knows this by now; they call the place Murder Meadow. It's exactly what we find written in the Psalms:

> *Let his farm become haunted*
> *So no one can ever live there.*

And also what was written later:

> *Let someone else take over his post.*

Acts 1:16-20

Then they prayed and held a vote. The vote went to Matthias, and he was counted with the eleven apostles. Peter, then, was the one who solved the first succession crisis in the Church. Note that he did so collaboratively!

A few days later came the powerful event of Pentecost. As Jesus had promised, the Holy Spirit descended upon the gathered community of disciples, filling them with clear knowledge and "bold confidence" to make known the name and Gospel of Jesus to the rest of the world. Peter was the first one to speak.

> *Peter said, "Change your life. Turn to God and be baptized, each of you, in the name of Jesus Christ, so your sins are forgiven. Receive the gift of the Holy Spirit. The promise is targeted to you and your children, but also to all who are far away—whomever, in fact, our Master God invites."*
>
> *He went on in this vein for a long time, urging them over and over, "Get out while you can; get out of this sick and stupid culture!"*
>
> *That day about three thousand took him at his word, were baptized and were signed up. They committed themselves to the teaching of the apostles, the life together, the common meal, and the prayers.*
>
> *Everyone around was in awe—all those wonders and signs done through the apostles! And all the believers lived in a*

wonderful harmony, holding everything in common. They sold whatever they owned and pooled their resources so that each person's need was met.

They followed a daily discipline of worship in the Temple followed by meals at home, every meal a celebration, exuberant and joyful, as they praised God. People in general liked what they saw. Every day their number grew as God added those who were saved.

Acts 2:38-47

So Peter became the first evangelist and missionary of the Church. He begins to preach and heal and is eventually arrested. Instead of denying Jesus, this time Peter defends him in no uncertain terms. One of the Jewish priests, named Gamaliel, prophetically says, "So I am telling you: Hands off these men! Let them alone. If this program or this work is merely human, it will fall apart, but if it is of God, there is nothing you can do about it—and you better not be found fighting against God!" (Acts 5:38-39).

Peter makes hard decisions—and so must we

Probably Peter's most important act of Church leadership had to do with the question of whether to admit Gentiles (non-Jews) into the Christian community. Again, in the long history of Judaism, the pagan Gentiles were seen as their nemesis, always tempting them away from worship and obedience to the true God. At the same time, the Old Testament prophets kept promising that someday the Gentiles would find their way to God via the prayers and good works of faithful Jews. Also, some saw the Messiah as the one who would open the door of faith to the Gentiles.

The first Christians lacked both the time and opportunity to reach out to the Gentiles. The breakthrough came from a double dream. First, a devout Gentile named Cornelius, a military man, had a vision of an angel who told him: Your prayers and almsgiving to the poor have found favor with God. Go now to the town of Joppa and ask for a man named Peter. At the same time, Peter had a strange vision during prayer. He saw a huge canvas coming down from heaven and filled with all sorts of animals considered unclean by Jewish Law. A voice told Peter to eat some of them, almost like telling him "Have a pork-chop!" Peter protested, "I have never eaten anything unclean." The voice replied, "What God has made clean, you are not to call unclean." This happened three times, leaving Peter deeply puzzled.

But just then, the friends of Cornelius arrived at Peter's door and said, "Captain Cornelius, a God-fearing man well-known for his fair play—ask any Jew in this part of the country—was commanded by a holy angel to get you and bring you to his house so he could hear what you had to say" (Acts 10:22).

So Peter and some of his friends from Joppa went with them to the home of Cornelius, who told him about his vision and the angel's instruction. Then Peter proceeded to tell the story of Jesus to Cornelius and his friends. As he was speaking, the Holy Spirit fell upon these Gentiles and they began praising God. Peter said to the friends who had accompanied him, "Do I hear any objections to baptizing these friends with water? They've received the Holy Spirit exactly as we did" (Acts 10:47). Since none of the followers of Jesus made any objections, Peter ordered that they be baptized immediately in the name of Jesus Christ. This incident was the beginning of an amazing development in the spread of Christianity: Jews and Gentiles both coming to faith in Jesus Christ. But it was not without some serious problems, as we will see later in the story of Paul.

What strikes me with particular force in these narratives about Peter is the remarkable change in him after Pentecost. He was always a sincere and good-hearted man, but he had two glaring faults.

First, he was impulsive, even hot-tempered, often speaking and acting without thinking. But now, through the transforming power of the Holy Spirit, he becomes much more thoughtful and collaborative. We saw how carefully and patiently he explained to the crowd at Pentecost what God had done through Jesus of Nazareth and how these events were the fulfillment of the Scriptures that the Jewish people reverenced. Moreover, he let his natural boldness work for him, leading him to heal the crippled man and to give all the credit to the power of Jesus rather than himself. He took the lead but sought the input of others in both the replacement of Judas and in the baptism of the Gentiles Cornelius and his companions.

Second, despite his external bravado, Peter often let himself be driven by fear. We saw that displayed during the storm on the lake and especially during Jesus' arrest and trial. But then, after Pentecost, this blustering but fear-driven man becomes a model of courage and confidence in the face of threats and imprisonment, telling his accusers in court, "We must obey God rather than you."

Some of us may be similarly endowed with a naturally impulsive temperament. That is not a necessary impediment to spiritual growth. In fact, it can be modified and channeled toward assertive action for facing and dealing with problems. It can also lead us to take initiative to bring about positive changes collaboratively in the workplace, in our church community, and even in our families. But that may require a good deal of prayer and self-honesty. Am I being driven by desire for power and control, or by genuine zeal for building up God's kingdom?

Likewise, if we have a tendency toward timidity, we need to take account of it rather than deny it. After all, the fear response is God-given, hard-wired into our genetic make-up. Its purpose is to protect us from rushing into dangerous situations. But it can also paralyze us. Think of the words "Do not be afraid." They appear in the Bible 365 times! (That's once for every day of the year!) I always say that God is obviously trying to tell us something. But I also say that even the Bible cannot command emotions. They have a life of their own, as well as a purpose. So when the Bible says "Do not be afraid," it cannot mean, "Never *feel* fear"; for that would be inhuman. The true meaning must be: Do not let fear drive your *choices*; for that is what God's grace is for.

People often make wrong choices, not so much out of evil intent, but out of fear. They steal out of fear of not having enough to care for themselves or their families. They lie out of fear of being embarrassed. They commit sexual sins from fear of being alone or unloved. You get the picture. This does not excuse them, but it can help us understand their behavior. So when the Bible says, "Do not be afraid," it really means: "Do the right thing, make the right choice—in spite of your fears. And I, God, will be with you to help you handle the consequences."

> We often make wrong choices, not so much out of evil intent, but out of fear.

That is what we saw in Peter after Pentecost. Strengthened by the Holy Spirit, he made difficult choices in face of his natural fears. And God was there to protect and assist him in dealing with the consequences of his choices. So it is with us. Often, we may have to make difficult choices, even amid great fears, because it is the right thing to do. God will be there to protect and assist us as well.

We know from history that Peter eventually traveled to Rome and became the undisputed leader of the Christian community there. While there, he wrote two letters to Christians scattered throughout the empire, encouraging them to remain faithful to Christ and to their vocation. When Emperor Nero began a persecution of the Christians, Peter was condemned to death by crucifixion, sometime between 64-67 A.D. According to a tradition, he asked to be crucified upside-down, since he felt he was not worthy to die in the same manner as his Lord Jesus.

We could do no better than to conclude this chapter by quoting from one of St. Peter's letters.

Summing up: Be agreeable, be sympathetic, be loving, be compassionate, be humble. That goes for all of you, no exceptions. No retaliation. No sharp-tongued sarcasm. Instead, bless—that's your job, to bless. You'll be a blessing and also get a blessing.

> *Whoever wants to embrace life*
>> *and see the day fill up with good,*
> *Here's what you do:*
>> *Say nothing evil or hurtful;*
> *Snub evil and cultivate good;*
>> *run after peace for all you're worth.*
> *God looks on all this with approval,*
>> *listening and responding well to what he's asked;*
> *But he turns his back*
>> *on those who do evil things.*

If with heart and soul you're doing good, do you think you can be stopped? Even if you suffer for it, you're still better off. Don't give the opposition a second thought. Through thick and thin, keep your hearts at attention, in adoration before Christ, your Master. Be ready to speak up and tell anyone who asks why you're living the way you are, and always with the utmost courtesy.

1 Peter 3:8-15

QUESTIONS FOR REFLECTION AND DISCUSSION

1. What one quality in St. Peter do you find most appealing? Why?

2. What are some of your fears, and how do you deal with them? Give examples.

3. Peter operated collaboratively on the issues of replacing Judas and baptizing Cornelius. Have you ever collaborated on a decision? If so, describe what happened.

4. Have you betrayed or denied someone? How did you feel afterward? How did you seek forgiveness?

5. What are the qualities you look for in a leader?

PAUL

Man Who Caught the Fire

Many of us *think* we don't like Paul. His letters are dense and intense and often filled with admonition. He seems very sure of himself. And he is exhausting to watch as he speeds around the Mediterranean Sea, trying to convert everyone at once. His persecution of the early Church only stopped after he was literally knocked off a horse, had a miraculous vision, and then became just as zealous for *our* side as he was for the *other* side. What are we to make of this complex and fascinating man?

We have a good deal of biographical information about Paul, yielding insights into his character. He was born in the city of Tarsus in the territory of Cilicia on the southern coast of modern-day Turkey somewhere between 5 and 10 A.D., placing his birth after Jesus and certainly later than most of the original disciples. He was one of a huge number of the so-called "Diaspora" (scattered Jews living in numerous locations throughout the Roman Empire). They were much more numerous than the Jews living in Palestine, their original homeland, which had been conquered and occupied by various invaders throughout the centuries. They had made legal arrangements with Greek and Roman rulers to protect their way of life, and they were allowed to gather freely for worship in their homes and synagogues. As a result, there were quasi-autonomous Jewish communities in nearly every major city of the Empire.

Tarsus was a major center of Greek culture, philosophy, and education. Paul learned Greek and studied Greek philosophy; he was much more learned than the apostles and disciples of Jesus who formed the first Christian communities. At the same time, he grew strong in his Jewish heritage, because the surrounding culture challenged rather than supported his religious beliefs. Being Jewish was tolerable but not fashionable.

Diaspora Jews maintained contact with their homeland. They made pilgrimages to Jerusalem, especially for the great feasts. They collected large sums of money for their fellow Jews in Palestine, many of whom were quite poor. They built their synagogues to face toward the Temple in Jerusalem. At the same time, they did not limit the presence of God to the Temple. They gathered for worship every Sabbath in the synagogue, where they prayed, sang, and listened to the Hebrew Scriptures.

The prevailing moods of the surrounding culture were anxiety and a certain feeling of helplessness. The pagan Gentiles lived in fear of displeasing the gods and felt the oppressive burden of Roman power. The Jews, on the other hand, yearned for the coming of the Messiah to deliver them, punish their enemies, and bless them for their fidelity.

Paul took his religion seriously—as we all should

Among the Jewish religious leaders there were two main factions. First were the Pharisees, to which Paul (whose Jewish name was Saul) belonged. They were laymen who arose some time after the Jews returned from their exile in Babylon around 500 B.C. Their main concern was to preserve Jewish identity in the midst of the Gentile world, especially by faithful observance of the Mosaic Law. They saw the Law not as a burden but as instruction for daily life. They believed their nation had been punished by God because of neglect and violations of the Law, so they drew up detailed regulations for observing the Sabbath, dietary laws, and tithing. They believed in resurrection and eternal life for Jews who were faithful. They were highly respected because they tried to make religion practical for daily life. By the time of Jesus, how-

ever, their beliefs and practices had gotten out of hand; they became rigid, smug, satisfied with themselves, and harsh and judg-
mental toward others.

The other main Jewish faction at the time was the Sadducees,
the priestly class who accepted only the written Law, not oral tradition. The Saducees denied the existence of angels and demons,
as well as resurrection and afterlife, and they no longer believed
in he coming of the Messiah. Unlike the Pharisees, they made ac-
commodations with the Gentile culture around them. They disappeared after the destruction of Jerusalem and the Temple in 70
A.D., right after Paul was martyred in Rome.

Saul studied the Law under the great rabbi Gamaliel. He never
became a rabbi himself, but he was able to claim: "I was so enthusiastic about the traditions of my ancestors that I advanced head
and shoulders above my peers in my career" (Galatians 1:14). To
support himself, he learned the trade of tent-making, using the
hair of mountain goats abundant in the mountains around Tarsus. This could be a profitable business at the time since the Roman armies occupying Asia Minor (Turkey) were in need of tents
for their troops.

At some point, Saul moved to Jerusalem and became a respected teacher of the Law. There he learned of the great controversies surrounding a certain Jesus of Nazareth and his followers,
eventually called "Christians," after the Greek word *Cristos*, which
means "Anointed One." Saul, of course, as a good Jewish scholar,
would have been naturally suspicious of anyone who claimed to
be the Messiah. A number of such people had come upon the
scene in Saul's lifetime, gathered groups of followers, but then
came to nothing. Surely, this Jesus was just one more Messianic
imposter.

Paul experiences a change of heart— and so must we

Along with other Jewish leaders at the time, Saul was determined to stamp out this new sect of Jews who had renounced their religion by claiming Jesus to be the long-awaited Messiah. Think about it from Saul's point of view: This ragtag group of mostly poor and illiterate Jews were claiming that some itinerant preacher from Galilee, of all places, had suddenly appeared on the scene, wandered around for few years, been crucified by the Romans, had risen from the dead (literally), and commissioned them (*them!*) to spread his vision of a new "kingdom of God" based purely on love. They were now gathering thousands of recruits to their crazy sect. What self-respecting religious leader would let *that* go on for long?

The flashpoint came with the arrest of Stephen, a Greek Christian who had been made a "deacon," a special leader, by the group. Stephen gave impassioned speeches in public, testifying to the life, crucifixion, and resurrection of Jesus of Nazareth. The Acts of the Apostles records a lengthy defense by Stephen in front of the Jewish leaders in which he connected the dots between Old Testament history and prophecy, and the life and teachings of Jesus (see Acts 7:1-53). The Jewish religious leaders were enraged by this speech, perhaps precisely because it was so effective, and they dragged him outside the city and stoned him to death. The text adds:

> *The ringleaders took off their coats and asked a young man named Saul to watch them.*
>
> *As the rocks rained down, Stephen prayed, "Master Jesus, take my life." Then he knelt down, praying loud enough for everyone to hear, "Master, don't blame them for this sin"—his last words. Then he died.*
>
> *Saul was right there, congratulating the killers.*
>
> *That set off a terrific persecution of the church in Jerusa-*

lem. The believers were all scattered throughout Judea and Samaria. All, that is, but the apostles. Good and brave men buried Stephen, giving him a solemn funeral—not many dry eyes that day!

And Saul just went wild, devastating the church, entering house after house after house, dragging men and women off to jail.

Acts 7:58–8:3

Shortly thereafter, Saul went to the high priest and obtained documents authorizing him to hunt down members of this new sect and bring them back to Jerusalem in chains. He headed north toward Damascus, where he heard there was a community of Christians. Then it happened.

When he got to the outskirts of Damascus, he was suddenly dazed by a blinding flash of light. As he fell to the ground, he heard a voice: "Saul, Saul, why are you out to get me?"

He said, "Who are you, Master?"

"I am Jesus, the One you're hunting down. I want you to get up and enter the city. In the city you'll be told what to do next."

His companions stood there dumbstruck—they could hear the sound, but couldn't see anyone—while Saul, picking himself up off the ground, found himself stone-blind. They had to take him by the hand and lead him into Damascus. He continued blind for three days. He ate nothing, drank nothing.

Acts 9:3-10

Saul had to be led into the city to the house of a Christian. Meanwhile, Jesus appeared to a Christian named Ananias and told him to find Saul. When Ananias objected that Saul was a notorious persecutor of Christians, Jesus replied, "Don't argue. Go! I have picked him as my personal representative to non-Jews and kings and Jews. And now I'm about to show him what he's in for—the hard suffering that goes with this job" (Acts 9:15-16).

So, Ananias came to Saul and told him that Jesus had sent him to restore his sight and bestow upon him the Holy Spirit. When Ananias baptized him, Saul recovered his sight and was able to eat and drink.

The Bible describes the conversion of Saul as a sudden and dramatic event. But I have always believed that it was a more gradual process. Recall that Saul was a truly devout and religious man. I believe he must have been deeply impressed by Stephen's speech in the presence of the Jewish religious leaders. Saul must have thought: This Greek Jew-turned-Christian really knows our Jewish history and theology. He claimed to see the heavens opened and Jesus standing at the right hand of God. What if that was true, not just a delusion? He did not curse when he was being stoned to death; in fact, he prayed for us: "Master, don't blame them for this sin" (Acts 7:60). On his subsequent trip to Damascus, after days of rounding up Christians and throwing them in jail, Saul must have been reflecting on what he had been doing. Moreover, during the three days of blindness, insomnia, and the inability to eat or drink, he must have been struggling inwardly: What does all this mean? Perhaps he was on the wrong side. The voice of Jesus had said, "Saul, Saul, why are you out to get me?" (Act 9:4)—not just "my followers." What could *that* mean? By the time Ananias came in, Paul was ready to become a Christian.

Conversion needs to be followed by ongoing spiritual growth.

Earlier in this book we reflected on our own spiritual awakening—how we came to awareness of our own desire to get serious about our spiritual life. But that awakening/conversion is only a beginning; it needs to be followed by ongoing spiritual growth. This is a more gradual process. Physicians, health care workers, technicians, managers, marketing persons—all types of workers need ongoing education to maintain excellence in their field. The same is equally true of our spiritual life. This is why we need to practice the classic spiritual disciplines. First among them is regular daily prayer. The very heart of our spiritual life is a personal relationship with Jesus Christ. Think about it: How do human relationships grow? Think of your wife or any of your friends. Basically, relationships grow by communication.

First, we need to spend time with the person. Notice the word *spend*. It's going to cost us something. Without spending time with a person, the relationship will die for lack of emotional oxygen. It is the same with our relationship with Christ. We need to spend some time each day in personal communication with him. This need not be long or intense. For instance, we could begin each day by thanking God for the gift of a new day and asking him to be with us and help us with the tasks of our day. In the evening we can again give thanks for the blessings of the day and ask forgiveness for ways that we may have been self-centered, irritable, uncaring, deceitful, and the like. Some brief reading from the Bible or other spiritual book can be a good help for prayer.

If we are going through a difficult time, our prayer will take the form of talking to the Lord about our problem(s) and asking for perspective on them as well as help in resolving them. And finally, when relationships are growing, people begin to care about what the other person cares about. I often ask people: Do you think Jesus cares about who becomes the next "American Idol?" Or wins the World Series? Or wins an Academy Award? Definitely not. What does he care about? That we are becoming less self-preoccupied and more caring of others; that we are devoted to our families; that we are conscientious in our jobs; that we are doing what we can to build a more just and peaceful society. That is ongoing conversion; that is spiritual growth. And it's a lifetime endeavor.

Paul starts to preach and is criticized—as we most likely will be too

Almost immediately after his conversion, Paul began preaching about Jesus in the Jewish synagogues in Damascus. It was around this time that he changed his name from Saul to Paul. The changing of one's name to signify a radical change is found elsewhere in the Bible (think about Abraham and Peter as only two examples.) Paul always began his evangelizing work by speaking to his fellow Jews first, since they were God's chosen people and had been waiting for the Messiah. Everyone in Damascus, Jews as well as Christians, were astonished at the change in him. They said, "Isn't this the man who wreaked havoc in Jerusalem among the believers? And didn't he come here to do the same thing—arrest us and drag us off to jail in Jerusalem for sentencing by the high priests?" (Acts 9:21).

After a while, Paul tells us in one of his letters, he went to Arabia for an unknown interlude (see Galatians 1:17). We do not know his purpose for this. Many scholars believe he went there as a kind of spiritual retreat, to strengthen his personal relationship with Christ and to reflect on the connections between his teachings and the writings of the Old Testament. Then he returned to Damascus and renewed his preaching. After a while, however, the Jewish leaders became alarmed at the number of people converting to Christianity. They devised a plot to kill Paul, but friends helped him to escape by hiding him in a large basket and lowering it through a hole in the city wall (see Acts 9:25). One of the moments of high action drama in the Bible!

From there, Paul made his way to Jerusalem to meet and confer with Peter for the very first time. It was three years since his conversion, yet this was the first time he had contacted the leaders of the nascent movement. He tried to join the Christian community there; but we read that "they were all afraid of him. They didn't trust him one bit" (Acts 9:26). But a Christian leader named Barnabas "took him under his wing. He introduced him to the apostles and stood up for him, told them how Saul had seen and spoken to the Master on the Damascus Road and how in Damascus itself he had laid his life on the line with his bold preaching in Jesus' name" (Acts 9:27). This reassurance from a trusted member of the group allowed Paul to continue his preaching, but he ran afoul of the Hellenists. These Greek Jews, who were at odds with the main group of Jewish Christians, plotted to kill him. Paul's friends took him to the seaport of Caesarea and shipped him back to Tarsus, his home town (see Acts 9:28-30). It's as if they were saying, "Paul, go home for a while and cool your jets!"

I have often thought about this incident, wondering how Paul dealt with this particular setback. Imagine this man, with all his learning and his new-found desire to proclaim Jesus as the Christ, being told "Take a leave of absence; you're benched." The Bible does not record Paul's thoughts or actions. No doubt he spent his time making tents, praying, and studying the Scriptures. He certainly must have felt hurt and rejected, but there is no indication of how he worked through his feelings. Recall that Jesus had warned of "the hard suffering that goes with this job" (Acts 9:16). Paul was probably ready to endure that from outsiders, but it must have been particularly painful coming from his fellow Christians.

Barnabas recruited Paul—as others will recruit us

We do not know how long Paul remained in Tarsus; it was probably at least a year. Meanwhile, exciting things were happening back in Antioch, another major city in Syria. Some Christian missionaries came to town and preached the Gospel of Jesus to fellow Jews. However, some of them also began speaking to the Gentiles:

> *God was pleased with what they were doing and put his stamp of approval on it—quite a number of the Greeks believed and turned to the Master.*
>
> *When the church in Jerusalem got wind of this, they sent Barnabas to Antioch to check on things. As soon as he arrived, he saw that God was behind and in it all. He threw himself in with them, got behind them, urging them to stay*

*with it the rest of their lives. He was a good man that way,
enthusiastic and confident in the Holy Spirit's ways. The community grew large and strong in the Master.*

*Then Barnabas went on to Tarsus to look for Saul. He found
him and brought him back to Antioch. They were there a
whole year, meeting with the church and teaching a lot of
people. It was in Antioch that the disciples were for the first
time called Christians.*

Acts 11:21-26

In other words, it was Barnabas who gave official approval
from Peter and James and the other members of the "hierarchy" in
Jerusalem for Paul and others to preach to the Gentiles. Recall that
Peter had already baptized the Gentile Cornelius and his servants
and thereby opened the door of faith to Gentiles. So the events in
Antioch were a logical extension of the principle: all sincere believers, Jews and Gentiles alike, were to be welcomed into the newly
named "Christian" Church. Something new was loosed on the
world, and there was no way to stop it. And Paul was once again in
the middle of it.

Next we have the first example in the New Testament of how
the early Christians took care of the poor and hungry in their
midst. A man named Agabus, who had the gift of prophecy, foretold that a severe famine was about to come over the land—which
actually happened during the reign of Emperor Claudius around
46 A.D. So the disciples in Antioch decided that each should
make a contribution, according to their ability, and send it to the
Christians in Jerusalem and other places in Palestine. They entrusted the collection to Barnabas and Paul, who delivered it to
Jerusalem. Paul once again had the opportunity to interact with
Peter and the other leaders in Jerusalem. This would prove to be
important later, when the early Church had to deal with some
basic issues.

Back in Antioch, the Holy Spirit was again stirring things up:

One day as they were worshiping God—they were also fasting as they waited for guidance—the Holy Spirit spoke: "Take Barnabas and Saul and commission them for the work I have called them to do."

So they commissioned them. In that circle of intensity and obedience, of fasting and praying, they laid hands on their heads and sent them off.

Acts 13:2-3

This was the beginning of Paul's three great missionary journeys, which transformed the Church from an insular Jewish sect to the universal religion it is today. This was the first specific call of foreign missionaries, and it is a tradition that continues to this day in the Church.

Any man who has ever been laid off from work or told he is no longer needed can identify with Paul in his forced return to Tarsus. I can still recall very vividly a time like this in my own life. I was 19 years old when I applied to join the Capuchin Order and was accepted as a novice. Halfway through that year, I was called in by the director and told that I needed to leave. Perhaps I had a vocation, the director told me, but right then I was not ready. I knew he was right. I was self-conscious and insecure. I had a bad stuttering problem, especially when I had to read or pray in public. Full of shame and sorrow, I had to call my parents and tell them I was coming home. This was the lowest point in my life.

I was able to get a job as a stock boy in a drugstore and began seeing a therapist for counseling. He told me I didn't have any major psychological problems; I just needed to develop self-confidence. I thought: That's like telling a drowning man, "What you need is to learn how to swim!" Obvious—but how to do it?

The therapist urged me to leave home and move to Milwaukee. He helped me find a residence hall with other young men and get a job as a shipping clerk. Next he urged me to continue my studies at Marquette University, which I did. I even began dating girls. Sure enough—my self-confidence began to grow. After eighteen months I decided to reapply for the novitiate and was accepted. Looking back, I could see that this setback was all part of God's plan. I developed a strong sense of empathy for people who are going through painful loss, confusion, failure, and other life stresses. To my surprise, after ordination my superiors asked me to obtain a doctorate in Counseling Psychology so I could help our own friars and other people. Clearly, God knew what he was doing.

Our setbacks can be occasions for grace and for personal and spiritual growth.

Like Paul, our setbacks can be occasions for grace and for personal and spiritual growth. But they can also become sources of bitterness and resentment. We cannot always prevent losses, failures, and unjust treatment, but we can choose our response toward them, whether negative or positive. Often it will take time to move from one to the other. Some people get stuck at the negative pole, continually ruminating about their misfortune and wearying others with their complaints. Others seek help in prayer and other spiritual resources. They manage to move from resentment to serenity. I have always liked the line in the song "Try to Remember" from *The Fantastiks*: "Deep in December it's good to remember: without a hurt, the heart is hollow." People who have suffered often have a great sense of compassion for those who are hurting; they are good to be around. This was Paul.

Paul has a tough start—as we sometimes do
First Missionary Journey (46-49 A.D.)

It seems Barnabas was the real leader on the first journey. He took his cousin John Mark along with Paul. Many consider this to be the same Mark who wrote the first Gospel under the tutelage of Peter, but then he was really a young man just starting out in public life.

"Sent off on their new assignment by the Holy Spirit" (Acts 13:4), the three missionaries' first stop was at the island of Cyprus in the Mediterranean. As usual, they began by preaching in the Jewish synagogues, but eventually they covered the whole island, ending at the pagan governor's court. Sergius had summoned them, "wanting to hear God's Word firsthand from them" (Acts 13:7). We need to recall here that there were many Gentiles who greatly admired the Jewish religion because of its beautiful worship and its high moral standards. But they were reluctant to convert to Judaism because of all the detailed regulations and especially because of the requirement of circumcision. The Jews gave these people the title "God-fearers," that is, pagans who reverenced the true God.

But Barnabas and Paul were opposed by a self-proclaimed Jewish magician named Bar-Jesus. He was a false prophet who tried to turn Sergius away from what Paul and Barnabas were saying. But Paul confronted him on his evil ways, afflicting him with temporary blindness. Sergius was convinced and became a Christian. At that point, John Mark left the mission and returned to Jerusalem. The Bible does not say why, but we have to assume there was some dissension between him and Paul.

From there, Barnabas and Paul sailed to Antioch in Pisidia (southern Turkey). They went to the synagogue and were invited to speak. This was common practice when Jewish visitors attended a service. Paul gave a long sermon, tracing the history of the Jewish people and leading up to Jesus' death and resurrection. Afterwards, a good number of Jews began to follow Barnabas and Paul.

> When the next Sabbath came around, practically the whole city showed up to hear the Word of God. Some of the Jews, seeing the crowds, went wild with jealousy and tore into Paul, contradicting everything he was saying, making an ugly scene.
>
> But Paul and Barnabas didn't back down. Standing their ground they said, "It was required that God's Word be spoken

*first of all to you, the Jews. But seeing that you want no part
of it—you've made it quite clear that you have no taste or in-
clination for eternal life—the door is open to all the outsiders.
And we're on our way through it, following orders, doing what
God commanded when he said,*

> *I've set you up
>   as light to all nations.
> You'll proclaim salvation
>   to the four winds and seven seas!"*

*When the non-Jewish outsiders heard this, they could hardly
believe their good fortune. All who were marked out for* real
life *put their trust in God—they honored God's Word by
receiving that life. And this Message of salvation spread like
wildfire all through the region.*

Acts 13:44-49

Then Paul and Barnabas moved on to Iconium, the capital of
ancient Lycaonia, at the foot of Mt. Taurus, halfway between Ephesus and Antioch. There they again made a great number of converts, both Jews and Gentiles. But after some time, a faction from
both groups plotted to stone them, so they fled to nearby Lystra.
There Paul healed a man who was crippled from birth. When the
Gentiles saw that, they thought Barnabas and Paul must be gods;
they even wanted to offer sacrifice to them. But the missionaries
calmed them down, telling them there is only one true God and
that it was God's power that had healed the lame man. Then some
Jews from Antioch and Iconium arrived and convinced the crowd
to stone Paul, leaving him for dead. "But as the disciples gathered
around him, he came to and got up. He went back into town and
the next day left with Barnabas for Derbe" (Acts 14:20). I always
think of this scene as a wonderful example of "the circle of care"
we Christians ought to provide when one of our members is hurting or in trouble.

Barnabas and Paul then arrived in the nearby town of Derbe, where they succeeded in making a considerable number of converts. Then they went back and revisited each of the towns where they had preached:

Paul and Barnabas handpicked leaders in each church. After praying—their prayers intensified by fasting—they presented these new leaders to the Master to whom they had entrusted their lives. Working their way back through Pisidia, they came to Pamphylia and preached in Perga. Finally, they made it to Attalia and caught a ship back to Antioch, where it had all started—launched by God's grace and now safely home by God's grace. A good piece of work.

On arrival, they got the church together and reported on their trip, telling in detail how God had used them to throw the door of faith wide open so people of all nations could come streaming in. Then they settled down for a long, leisurely visit with the disciples.

Acts 14:23-26

Paul takes on his superiors—
as we should at times
Council of Jerusalem (50 A.D.)

Meanwhile, a serious controversy had arisen among the Christian community, one that threatened the very unity of the Church. Some Jewish converts began insisting that the Gentile converts could not be saved unless they were circumcised. Barnabas and Paul strongly objected to this idea, insisting that everyone is saved by the grace of Jesus Christ, not by observance of the Law. Everyone agreed to bring the matter to the attention of the Church leaders in Jerusalem, mainly Peter and James. The ultimate question was this: Was Christianity to become a separate religion or remain a sect within Judaism?

The apostles and leaders called a special meeting to consider the matter. The arguments went on and on, back and forth, getting more and more heated. Then Peter took the floor: "Friends, you well know that from early on God made it quite plain that he wanted the pagans to hear the Message of this good news and embrace it—and not in any secondhand or roundabout way, but firsthand, straight from my mouth. And God, who can't be fooled by any pretense on our part but always knows a person's thoughts, gave them the Holy Spirit exactly as he gave him to us. He treated the outsiders exactly as he treated us, beginning at the very center of who they were and working from that center outward, cleaning up their lives as they trusted and believed him.

"So why are you now trying to out-god God, loading these new believers down with rules that crushed our ancestors and crushed us, too? Don't we believe that we are saved because the Master Jesus amazingly and out of sheer generosity moved to save us just as he did those from beyond our nation? So what are we arguing about?"

There was dead silence. No one said a word. With the room quiet, Barnabas and Paul reported matter-of-factly on the miracles and wonders God had done among the other nations through their ministry. The silence deepened; you could hear a pin drop.

Acts 15:6-13

James, who was recognized as the head of the Church in Jerusalem, basically concurred with Paul and Barnabas. The assembly concluded by composing a letter to be read to the community in Antioch (and, by extension, any place where the controversy was troubling people), saying that all baptized Christians, whether Jews or Gentiles, were free from the requirement of circumcision and observance of the Mosaic Law. The Ten Commandments, of course, remain in force because they were endorsed by Jesus himself. Then Barnabas and Paul returned, like heroes, to Antioch. "On arrival, they gathered the church and read the letter. The people were greatly relieved and pleased. Judas and Silas, good preachers both of them, strengthened their new friends with many words of courage and hope. Then it was time to go home. They were sent off by their new friends with laughter and embraces all around to report back to those who had sent them" (Acts 15:30-33).

The meeting in Jerusalem is often regarded as the First Ecumenical Council of the church. It was truly an example of fraternal dialogue under the guidance of the Holy Spirit. There was no longer any doubt that Christianity was a religion separate from Judaism, though its roots were deep in Jewish history and tradition. We Christians must never forget our ties with our Jewish brothers and sisters, nor lose our reverence for their beliefs and practices. They are truly our spiritual ancestors in the faith.

When we look at the intense missionary activity of Barnabas and Paul, we can't help asking, "What was driving them?" Most of their travel was on foot. They never knew where they would be staying or how they would be received. Practically everywhere they went, they encountered opposition, hostility, and even physical injury. They had to be spiritually strong men. But they would say: We are simply being obedient to the commission we all received from the Lord Jesus at his ascension into heaven: "God authorized and commanded me to commission you: Go out and train everyone you meet, far and near, in this way of life, marking them by baptism in the threefold name: Father, Son, and Holy Spirit. Then instruct them in the practice of all I have commanded you. I'll be with you as you do this, day after day after day, right up to the end of the age" (Matthew 28:19-20).

Christianity is a missionary religion by its very nature. Our faith is a gift that is not meant merely for ourselves; we are called to share it. Pope Francis never tires of saying that a church that just stays in the sanctuary and does not go out into the streets will become a sick church! We will reflect more later on how we all need to become more evangelizing, both as individuals and as parishes and dioceses.

We also see how the apostles' missionary efforts involved

failure and suffering. In one of his letters, Paul tells of how he had to endure imprisonments, beatings, being stoned, being shipwrecked, suffering from hunger, cold, and sleepless nights (see 2 Corinthians 12:23-27). Our own trials are usually not that dramatic; still, they can test our faith and our stamina. "Where is God in all this?" we sometimes lament. Often there is no clear answer. We have to plod on, groping our way by sheer faith that love will sustains us. We fall back on that drum-beat promise of God: "Fear not. I am with you. I will not abandon you." We continue to believe that our God is a faithful God.

Finally, we learn from the dispute over the Gentile converts that the early Church developed a structure for resolving such controversies. Instead of splitting up into rival factions, they came together in dialogue, trusting in the guidance of the Holy Spirit whom Jesus promised would "take you by the hand and guide you into all the truth there is" (John 16:13). The story also shows that the Church had already formed a basic hierarchical order, with Peter (along with James and several elders) having supreme authority, even over such prominent leaders as Barnabas and Paul.

Paul and Barnabas have a falling out— and sometimes we will too
Second Missionary Journey (49-52 A.D.)

After the controversy regarding the Gentile converts had been settled, Paul suggested that he and Barnabas revisit the places they had evangelized to see how the Christians were doing. Barnabas wanted to take John Mark along, but Paul objected because the young man had bailed out on their previous journey; this seemed fickle to Paul. Their disagreement was so sharp that the two friends separated: Barnabas took John Mark and sailed for Cyprus while Paul chose Silas (also called Silvanus) and took the land route through Syria and Asia Minor (Turkey). We see from this incident that even good people can have conflicts. This is the last we hear of Barnabas in the Bible. According to tradition, he suffered martyrdom on Cyprus.

Paul and Silas returned to the towns of Derbe and Lystra. There they met a disciple named Timothy. He was highly regarded by the people there, so Paul asked him to accompany them. As they traveled from city to city, they shared with the Christians the decisions made at the Council of Jerusalem. The Bible adds: "Day after day the congregations became stronger in faith and larger in size" (Acts 16:5). They moved on through Galatia (northern Turkey) and established churches there. One of Paul's letters is addressed to the Galatians.

One night, Paul had a vision. A man from Macedonia stood before him and said, "Come over to Macedonia and help us" (Acts 16:9). This was another key moment for the early Church. Macedonia was in Greece, on the continent of Europe. The Gospel was reaching into the very heart of the Roman Empire. The first place they stopped was in the city of Philippi, made famous by Alexander the Conqueror who named the town after his father, Philip of Macedon. The missionaries went to the river bank on the Sabbath where local Jews gathered for prayer. They spoke with some women there, one of whom was Lydia. She was a Gentile "God-fearer" and a wealthy woman. The Bible says, "As she listened with intensity to what was being said, the Master gave her a trusting heart—and she believed!" (Acts 16:14). Afterwards, she and her household were baptized—the first Christian converts in Europe.

It might be time to address the issue of Paul's view of equality among Christians, especially between men and women. Paul was a product of his times, just as we all are. Some of his comments on the proper role of women in marriage or in public life are formed by his time and culture. But the story of Lydia and other women in the story of Paul show that he viewed them as equal partners in his mission. More than that, he proposed an even more radical formula for Christians: "In Christ's family there can be no division into Jew and non-Jew, slave and free, male and female. Among us you are all equal. That is, we are all in a common relationship with Jesus Christ" (Galatians 3:28). So anyone who uses Paul to argue for unequal treatment among various groups of Christians is most likely barking up the wrong tree.

To show how Paul viewed women, see how he handled one who was being exploited. The missionaries encountered a girl who was a slave and a fortune-teller. She kept following them and crying out to the people about them. Finally, Paul cast the evil spirit out of her, but that brought trouble. The girl's owners, who were used to making money from her fortune-telling, realized they had lost their source of profit. They seized Paul and Silas and told the authorities they were disturbing the peace. The authorities then beat them with rods and threw them into prison.

That night, Paul and Silas were singing hymns to God in their prison cell. Suddenly, an earthquake shook the prison so badly that all the doors flew open and the prisoners' chains were pulled loose. When the jailer saw this, he drew his sword and was about to kill himself (perhaps thinking he would be blamed for the prisoners' escape), but Paul shouted, "Don't do that! We're all still here! Nobody's run away!" (Acts 16:28). The jailer fell to his knees and said, "Sirs, what do I have to do to be saved, to really live?" (Acts 16:30). Paul shared with him and his family the story of Jesus, and all of them asked to be baptized. After the jailer took them into his house and shared a good meal with them, Paul and Silas went back to Lydia's house, where they shared with the Christians there all that had happened.

When trouble began to brew again, their friends took Paul to the seacoast, where he boarded a ship for Athens. Silas and Timothy stayed behind. During the four- to five-day voyage, he had time to pray and think through his strategy. After all, this was the moment he had been waiting for—the opportunity to speak to the intellectual and cultural elite of the civilized world.

Paul began by wandering around downtown Athens. He was disturbed by the sight of so many statues of pagan gods and goddesses. He talked with people on the street and was eventually invited to address a gathering of curious townsfolk who wondered what kind of philosophy he was following. Paul welcomed the opportunity. He delivered a superb lecture, beginning with quotes from of some the Athenians' own philosophers and poets. He pointed to the beauty and order of the created world, and then moved on to the existence of a personal Creator God who sent his own Son Jesus into the world to show us how God wants us to live. Paul explained that Jesus' teachings aroused opposition among some, who condemned him to death. But God raised Jesus from death, giving the hope of eternal life for all who believe in him. Pauls speech fell flat, and the Athenians walked away, muttering that resurrection from the dead is simply impossible (see Acts 18:16-34).

Paul was deeply disappointed that he had failed to convert the cultured elite at Athens, a failure that hold some important lessons for us. Despite careful preparation, our best efforts will not always succeed—and it is not always our fault. We saw how carefully Paul had thought out his strategy and how skillfully he had begun with the people's own experience of searching for the divine, even quoting their own authors. The speech was a masterpiece of rhetoric. But, in the end, the materialist philosophy of his hearers could not deal with the resurrection of Christ. The truth is that sometimes people are simply not ready to accept a spiritual or religious message, especially in a secularist culture like our own. We can only present the truth of the Gospel in the most attractive way we can imagine. In the end, our listeners must be receptive, and that is not within our control. If we have given our best, we can be at peace.

Paul then left Athens and traveled to Corinth. The two cities could not have been more opposite: Athens, the city of culture and learning; Corinth, a seaport town filled with taverns and houses of prostitution. Paul must have thought: If the Gospel was rejected in Athens, how can it possibly be received in Corinth? Yet, when we read Paul's letters to the Corinthians, it appears that he succeeded very well. I have often thought that Paul clearly changed his approach at Corinth. Notice that at Athens he had completely passed over the crucifixion and death of Jesus; he went right to the resurrection. Could it be that, by omitting the story of Jesus' suffering and dying for us, the Athenians could feel no empathy or solidarity with him? At Corinth, however, Paul made the cross of Jesus front and center:

> *You'll remember, friends, that when I first came to you to let you in on God's master stroke, I didn't try to impress you with polished speeches and the latest philosophy. I deliberately kept it plain and simple: first Jesus and who he is; then Jesus and what he did—Jesus crucified.*
>
> *I was unsure of how to go about this, and felt totally inadequate—I was scared to death, if you want the truth of it—and so nothing I said could have impressed you or anyone else. But the Message came through anyway. God's Spirit and God's power did it, which made it clear that your life of faith is a response to God's power, not to some fancy mental or emotional footwork by me or anyone else.*
>
> *1 Corinthians 2:1-5*

Paul's message in Corinth found a welcome. "In the course of listening to Paul, a great many Corinthians believed and were baptized. One night the Master spoke to Paul in a dream: "Keep it up, and don't let anyone intimidate or silence you. No matter what happens, I'm with you and no one is going to be able to hurt you. You have no idea how many people I have on my side in this city." That was all he needed to stick it out. He stayed another year and a half, faithfully teaching the Word of God to the Corinthians" (Acts 18:8-11).

Here is a powerful lesson for us: Never be ashamed to speak of the cross. It always bothers me when someone wears it merely as an ornament, without reference to Christ or his suffering and death for us. However, it can often be a good conversation-starter for evangelization: "I see you're wearing a cross; are you a Christian?" If the answer is yes, we can go on to ask what church the person belongs to; and often we discover they are not involved in any church community, are non-practicing Catholics, or are looking for a spiritual home. Further conversation may reveal that they are not entirely happy about being spiritual loners and are open to reconnect with Christ or with a church. In any case, what have we lost if we have this conversation with others? It is amazing how many spiritual seekers are out there and are willing to talk about their situation. They will not make the first move; but if someone opens the door (without being pushy) they are sometimes willing to walk through.

It is amazing how many spiritual seekers are willing to talk about their situation.

Paul settled in Corinth for eighteen months. He made friends with a Jewish Christian couple named Priscilla and Aquila, fellow tent-makers. Paul stayed at their house, worked with them, and continued his mission of preaching. When he left for to Ephesus, an important seaport town in Turkey, he placed Priscilla and Aquila in charge of the Christian church in Corinth. Then he returned to Antioch, giving a report of his experiences to the community.

An interesting insight from Paul's missionary activity is that he did not hesitate to form lay leaders and invest them with authority over church communities. The outstanding examples of lay leadership were Priscilla and Aquila who mentored a Jew named Apollos. He had a wonderful gift for speaking. After receiving instruction, Aquila, Apollos was baptized and served as a Christian evangelist. Today's Catholic Church has rediscovered this tradition of lay leadership and ministry, though it has been present in Protestant churches for centuries.

Paul stirs things up—which we need
to be willing to do
Third Missionary Journey (54-57 A.D.)

About two years later, Paul wanted to revisit some of the churches he had helped to establish. He went first to Ephesus. Once again he began speaking in the Jewish synagogue; but when some of them disparaged what he was saying, he withdrew to a lecture hall where he held daily discussions with both Jews and Greeks. They came from all over the province of Asia Minor and many were converted to Christ (see Acts 19:8-12).

Paul then left for Macedonia in Greece. There he visited some of the towns he had previously evangelized and encouraged the Christians to remain steadfast in their faith. He crossed back into Asia Minor and did the same there. During the week he spent in Troas, a humorous incident took place. The night before he was to leave, Paul gave a very lengthy speech in an upstairs room. A young man named Eutychus was sitting on the window sill; at one point he became drowsy and fell out of the window, three stories down. When the people picked him up, he was dead. But Paul embraced him and said, "No more crying. There's life in him yet."

They took the boy away alive. Was he actually dead, and had Paul revived him? Or were the people mistaken about his death? Perhaps the boy had just had the wind knocked out of him. The Bible does not say. In any case, Eutychus could be considered the patron saint of all men who fall asleep during sermons!

Paul went on to Miletus, about 35 miles south of Ephesus, where he had asked the presbyters (elders) from Ephesus to meet him. He proceeded to give a very touching address to them and the others gathered there. He said he is being impelled by the Holy Spirit to go to Jerusalem, even though the Spirit had been warning him that hardships and even imprisonment are awaiting him.

But that matters little. What matters most to me is to finish what God started: the job the Master Jesus gave me of letting everyone I meet know all about this incredibly extravagant generosity of God.

And so this is good-bye. You're not going to see me again, nor I you, you whom I have gone among for so long proclaiming the news of God's inaugurated kingdom. I've done my best for you, given you my all, held back nothing of God's will for you.

"Now it's up to you. Be on your toes—both for yourselves and your congregation of sheep. The Holy Spirit has put you in charge of these people—God's people they are—to guard and protect them. God himself thought they were worth dying for."
Acts 20:24-28

Paul ended his farewell by reminding them that he had always lived simply and made his own living. Then he reminded them of something Jesus had said, "I've never, as you so well know, had any taste for wealth or fashion. With these bare hands I took care of my own basic needs and those who worked with me. In everything I've done, I have demonstrated to you how necessary it is to work on behalf of the weak and not exploit them. You'll not likely go wrong here if you keep remembering that our Master said, 'You're far happier giving than getting'" (Acts 20:33-35).

"It is more blessed to give than to receive." This famous saying attributed to Jesus is one example of the many sayings and events handed down by oral tradition but not recorded in the Scriptures. At the end of Paul's speech, everyone knelt down and prayed, many of them weeping at the thought that they will never see Paul again. Then Paul and his companions returned by sea to Palestine. There he was warned by a number of different disciples not to go to Jerusalem. He replied, "Why all this hysteria? Why do you insist on making a scene and making it even harder for me? You're looking at this backward. The issue in Jerusalem is not what they do to me, whether arrest or murder, but what the Master Jesus does through my obedience. Can't you see that?" (Acts 21:13).

St. Luke, the writer of Acts and a Greek Christian who by this time was traveling with Paul, ends with a personal note, "We saw that we weren't making even a dent in his resolve, and gave up. 'It's in God's hands now,' we said. 'Master, you handle it'" (Acts 21: 14). This is a touching moment in Scripture indeed.

One final connection with today. Paul consistently showed remarkable courage in the face of opposition and persecution. As we saw with St. Peter, Paul had to endure not only insults but also stoning, beating, and imprisonment. In one of his letters he elaborates on these sufferings.

> I've worked much harder, been jailed more often, beaten up more times than I can count, and at death's door time after time. I've been flogged five times with the Jews' thirty-nine lashes, beaten by Roman rods three times, pummeled with rocks once. I've been shipwrecked three times, and immersed in the open sea for a night and a day. In hard traveling year in and year out, I've had to ford rivers, fend off robbers, struggle with friends, struggle with foes. I've been at risk in the city, at risk in the country, endangered by desert sun and sea storm, and betrayed by those I thought were my brothers. I've known drudgery and hard labor, many a long and lonely night without sleep, many a missed meal, blasted by the cold, naked to the weather.
>
> 2 Corinthians 11:23-27

Paul continually relied on those comforting words he heard from Jesus in a vision one night in Corinth: "Keep it up, and don't let anyone intimidate or silence you. No matter what happens, I'm with you and no one is going to be able to hurt you. You have no idea how many people I have on my side in this city" (Acts 18:9-10). Even though he knew he would face trial and possibly even death, he insisted on going to Jerusalem, because that is where the Spirit of God was leading him.

One of the gifts of the Holy Spirit is fortitude—the courage to do what we know needs to be done. Catholics believe that gift is conferred in the sacrament of Confirmation; it is also the fruit of prayer. It enables us to deal with our fears. Not that we will no longer *feel* afraid, since that is a physiological reaction of our autonomic nervous system. Rather, fortitude is the courage to do the right thing *in spite* of our fears. As I said earlier, too often we allow our fears to drive our choices. We're afraid to say, "I don't like that kind of talk" when people are telling trashy jokes or stories. We're afraid to say, "No, I won't cover up or lie for you." We too easily give in to our children's demands because we don't want them to hassle us or dislike us. We're afraid to challenge our friend who is drinking too much or cheating on his spouse. We're afraid to tell our boss we would rather not work on Sunday because we want to keep the Lord's day sacred. The virtue of fortitude strengthens us to make the right spiritual and moral decisions in face of our fears. Paul had fortitude to spare!

Paul's journey comes to an end—as will ours

When Paul finally arrived in Jerusalem, he was warmly welcomed by the Christians there and delivered to them the collection he had taken up from the other churches to help the community in Jerusalem. The next day, he went to visit James and the other leaders; they told him there were rumors among the Jews that he had been teaching the Jewish Christians and Gentile converts that they are not bound to observe the Law of Moses. They were very disturbed. In fact, Paul had simply been informing his converts about the decisions of the Council of Jerusalem: that they were not bound to circumcision and all the dietary laws, except law prohibiting meat sacrificed to pagan idols, meat of strangled animals, and drinking blood (see Acts 15:29). Paul always taught them that they were still bound by the Ten Commandments and the other moral precepts of the Law. He also allowed both Jew and Gentile converts to observe other practices of the Old Law if they freely chose to do so.

So Paul asked permission to speak to the crowd. When they

heard him speaking in Hebrew, they quieted down. Paul then proceeded to share with them how he had been a devout Jew, a zealous teacher of the Law, and a persecutor of Christians. But when he had a vision of the risen Christ, he was convinced in his conscience that he had to become his disciple. This testimony only enraged the crowd, and they began clamoring for his death. Then the Roman commander removed Paul to safety and interrogated him under threat of scourging. When Paul told the officer that he was a Roman citizen, the commander backed off. Instead, he turned Paul over to the Jewish court, the Sanhedrin (see Acts 22). This whole episode is reminiscent to me of how Jesus was sent back and forth from Pilate to Caiaphas to Herod the night of his trial.

In the courtroom, Paul made a very ingenious move. He knew that some of his accusers were Pharisees while others were Sadducees, with deep religious divisions between them, as I noted earlier. One big point of contention was that the Pharisees believed in resurrection of the dead, while the Sadducees did not. So Paul spoke up and said, "Friends, I am a stalwart Pharisee from a long line of Pharisees. It's because of my Pharisee convictions—the hope and resurrection of the dead—that I've been hauled into this court" (Acts 23:6). That provoked a major argument between the two factions: the Pharisees asking for Paul's release, while the Sadducees demanded his death. Fearing a riot, the commander ordered his troops to rescue Paul and place him in protective custody. That night Jesus appeared to Paul and said, "It's going to be all right. Everything is going to turn out for the best. You've been a good witness for me here in Jerusalem. Now you're going to be my witness in Rome!" (Acts 23:11).

The next day the commander, hearing that some Jews were plotting to kill Paul, ordered him to be taken under military guard to the Roman governor (Felix) in Caesarea. Felix listened to the accusations against Paul made by the Jewish high priest: "We've found this man time and again disturbing the peace, stirring up riots against Jews all over the world, the ringleader of a seditious sect called Nazarenes. He's a real bad apple, I must say. We caught him trying to defile our holy Temple and arrested him. You'll be able to verify all these accusations when you examine him yourself" (Acts 24:5-8).

Then Paul very calmly gave his defense, eloquent as always. At the end, Festus postponed a decision. Meanwhile, he would often speak privately with Paul, hoping he would offer a bribe (see Acts 24:10-26). Paul was kept in custody in Caesarea for two full years. During that time, Felix was succeeded by another governor, Festus. Again, the Jewish leaders from Jerusalem laid out their accusations against Paul while he insisted he has committed no crime, either against Jewish or Roman law. Festus asked him if he was willing to return to Jerusalem for trial. But Paul insisted: "I'm standing at this moment before Caesar's bar of justice, where I have a perfect right to stand. And I'm going to keep standing here. I've done nothing wrong to the Jews, and you know it as well as I do. If I've committed a crime and deserve death, name the day. I can face it. But if there's nothing to their accusations—and you know there isn't—nobody can force me to go along with their nonsense. We've fooled around here long enough. I appeal to Caesar" (Acts 25:10-11).

A few days later, Festus had some visitors, King Agrippa and his sister Bernice. Agrippa was a petty figurehead king the Romans had put over a small area of northern Palestine. Festus decided to pass Paul's case over to Agrippa, and the king agreed, probably mostly out of curiosity and to be able to exercise a little power. So, for the third time in the Book of Acts, Paul told the story of his previous life as a Pharisee and of his conversion on the way to Damascus. The story continues.

That was too much for Festus. He interrupted with a shout: "Paul, you're crazy! You've read too many books, spent too much time staring off into space! Get a grip on yourself, get back in the real world!"

But Paul stood his ground. "With all respect, Festus, Your Honor, I'm not crazy. I'm both accurate and sane in what I'm saying. The king knows what I'm talking about. I'm sure that nothing of what I've said sounds crazy to him. He's known all about it for a long time. You must realize that this wasn't done behind the scenes. You believe the prophets, don't you, King Agrippa? Don't answer that—I know you believe."

But Agrippa did answer: "Keep this up much longer and you'll make a Christian out of me!"

Paul, still in chains, said, "That's what I'm praying for, whether now or later, and not only you but everyone listening today, to become like me—except, of course, for this prison jewelry!"

The king and the governor, along with Bernice and their advisors, got up and went into the next room to talk over what they had heard. They quickly agreed on Paul's innocence, saying, "There's nothing in this man deserving prison, let alone death."

Agrippa told Festus, "He could be set free right now if he hadn't requested the hearing before Caesar."

Acts 26:24-32

So Paul's legal gambit had backfired. Along with some other prisoners, he was put on a ship bound for Italy. By this time, it was late in the year, not a good time for sailing. In fact, Paul warned the crew that they were risking all their lives, but the centurion followed the advice of the pilot and the owner of the ship. They set sail, hoping to reach a port in Crete where they could wait out the winter.

They began with a gentle south wind, but before long they ran into a heavy storm. They were pounded by the wind and rain so violently that they had to throw some of the cargo overboard. Then Paul gathered everyone together and said: "Friends, you really should have listened to me back in Crete. We could have avoided all this trouble and trial. But there's no need to dwell on that now. From now on, things are looking up! I can assure you that there'll not be a single drowning among us, although I can't say as much for the ship—the ship itself is doomed. Last night God's angel stood at my side, an angel of this God I serve, saying to me, 'Don't give up, Paul. You're going to stand before Caesar yet—and everyone sailing with you is also going to make it.' So, dear friends, take heart. I believe God will do exactly what he told me. But we're going to shipwreck on some island or other" (Acts 27:21-26).

And so it was. The sailors ran the ship aground on the island of Malta, and everyone on board reached shore safely. Three months later, Paul and the others were able to board another ship. Eventually, they arrived at the port of Puteoli, where Paul was met by a group of Christians and stayed with them for seven days, after which he arrived in Rome. We are not told of any court hearing for him; only that "they let Paul live in his own private quarters with a soldier who had been assigned to guard him" (Acts 28:16). In other words, he was kept under house arrest but was able to receive visitors.

Paul could never stop evangelizing. Three days after he arrived in Rome, he called together the Jewish leaders and shared with them the story of his troubles in Jerusalem, his arrest, and his appeal to the emperor of Rome because he was a Roman citizen. The leaders arranged a day when they could bring other Jews to listen to him. We read that a great number came. "Paul talked to them all day, from morning to evening, explaining everything involved in the kingdom of God, and trying to persuade them all about Jesus by pointing out what Moses and the prophets had written about him. Some of them were persuaded by what he said, but others refused to believe a word of it" (Acts 28:23-24).

The Book of Acts ends with these words: "Paul lived for two years in his rented house. He welcomed everyone who came to visit. He urgently presented all matters of the kingdom of God. He explained everything about Jesus Christ. His door was always open" (Acts 28:30-31).

Many scholars, but not all, believe that Paul's letter to the Philippians was written during his house arrest in Rome. If so, his statements would be most revealing:

I want to report to you, friends, that my imprisonment here has had the opposite of its intended effect. Instead of being squelched, the Message has actually prospered. All the soldiers here, and everyone else, too, found out that I'm in jail because of this Messiah. That piqued their curiosity, and now they've learned all about him. Not only that, but most of the followers of Jesus here have become far more sure of themselves in the faith than ever, speaking out fearlessly about God, about the Messiah.

It's true that some here preach Christ because with me out of the way, they think they'll step right into the spotlight. But the others do it with the best heart in the world. One group is motivated by pure love, knowing that I am here defending the Message, wanting to help. The others, now that I'm out of the picture, are merely greedy, hoping to get something out of it for themselves. Their motives are bad. They see me as their competition, and so the worse it goes for me, the better—they think—for them.

Philippians 1:12-17

This is the mature Paul. He is not troubled if others are gaining more attention or recognition than he is. All that matters is that Jesus and his Gospel are being proclaimed. This is a sobering reminder for Church ministers not to get caught up in petty rivalries or jealousies.

It seems probable that after two years of house arrest, Paul left Rome and revisited some of his former communities, especially Ephesus, Philippi, and Corinth. The early church historian, Eusebius of Caesarea, says that Paul was imprisoned in Rome a second time and that he was martyred under the emperor Nero, probably in 67 A.D., near the end of Nero's reign. He was buried at or near the site of the present-day Basilica of St. Paul-Outside-the-Walls, a beautiful church and a favorite place of pilgrimage to this day.

QUESTIONS FOR REFLECTION OR DISCUSSION

1. What do you like most about St. Paul? Why?

2. How do you overcome disappointment and failure? Give a real example from your life when you were able to do so.

3. Have you had falling outs with colleagues at work? What happened and how were things resolved?

4. When you think about your own death, what is it that you want to make sure you accomplish in this life? Make a list and share it with others.

5. Reflect on Paul's relationships with others, including fellow apostles, colleagues on mission, lay men and women in the churches he founded. What lessons do you want to learn from him?

EPILOGUE

You Go, Guys

It is no secret that many Christians, and especially we Catholic men, have lost our evangelizing fervor. There are historical and cultural reasons for this, mainly the fact that immigrant Catholics wanted to be accepted into American society. They lived their faith, but were reluctant to talk about it. That is how our dads were, and that is how we are. A similar tendency has also developed among the mainline Protestant churches, with the result that evangelism in this country has been identified almost exclusively with the Evangelical and Pentecostal churches.

Study after study has shown that the mainline churches are losing members, while Evangelical, Pentecostal, and so-called "non-denominational" churches are growing. A major factor has been the increasingly secular character of American society. Economic prosperity and personal fulfillment have become stronger values than religious commitment for a growing number of people. They may still believe in God, but they no longer feel the need to belong to a church community. "I'm spiritual but not religious" is the slogan many use to explain their absence from church life, along with "We're busy pursuing the good life."

As a result of all this, however, there is a renewed interest and desire among Catholics to reclaim the churches' evangelizing mission. The wake-up call came first from Pope Paul VI back in 1975 with his encyclical *On Evangelization in the Modern World.* When I read that document, it was truly life-changing. I must confess that I find most papal documents ponderous and hard to plow through, but this one was inspiring. It had passion and fire. I found myself saying, "I *have* to do something with this." So I began reading, and taking courses and workshops on evangelization. Pope John Paul II continued the direction in his World Youth Days and his call for "a new evangelization." Eventually I began teaching it in the seminary and giving programs for parish groups. I also wrote a book, *Reclaim the Fire: A Parish Guide for Evangelization* (ACTA Publications, 2009).

We Catholic men sometimes have skewed notions of evangelization. We perceive it as having to go up to people and say, "Are you saved?" Or "Have you accepted Jesus Christ as your personal Savior?" Or going from door-to-door and asking people if they are going to church. This is not the Catholic approach. There are gentle, respectful ways to evangelize.

There are gentle, respectful ways to evangelize.

First, evangelization means *appreciating* our faith and trying to deepen it. This includes the things we saw earlier in this book: regular prayer, reading the Bible and other spiritual resources, regular attendance at worship, studying and learning more about our faith, and celebrating the sacraments.

Second, evangelization means *living* our faith by our example. How do you think the early church grew so fast? There were very few mass conversions, other than the first Pentecost, when 3,000 received baptism. After that, it was mostly a matter of one-to-one connections. Christians *lived* their faith; were devoted to their families; were conscientious in their jobs; did not go along with the sinful practices of the pagans around them; took care of the poor and sick in their midst; and did it all with a spirit of joy and peacefulness. Soon, their Jewish and pagan neighbors would ask, "What's happened to you—you've changed." The Christian would reply, "You're right—I've come to know Jesus Christ. The other person may say, "Well, tell me about him." And the Christian would tell the story of Jesus and how it changed his or her life. Then, if the other was touched by God's grace, they would say, "That's what I'm looking for—how do I find it?" The Christian would answer with a simple invitation: "Come to the catechumen meetings and find out more; I'll go with you." That would eventually lead to baptism and membership in the church community.

Third, evangelization means *sharing* our faith. This usually begins not with talking but with listening. Someone confides in us their problem at work, in their family, with their health, or with a relationship, or so on. We listen attentively; not trying to solve the problem necessarily, because usually we can't. We don't need to talk theology or even about the Bible. The simplest way to respond, after making sure we understand what the other is saying, is just to share our own experience: how our faith in God and our membership in the church community has helped us, changed us, made a positive difference in our life, helped us get through a crisis or tough time, and gave us a sense of purpose. The marvelous thing about this is that nobody can argue with us. They can't say, "Nah, that didn't happen!" Yes, it did. The other person may not be ready to believe in Christ or join your church right away. But they will think about what we shared; and if God's grace touches them, they may begin to take some steps toward that goal. That's why I always urge people who have these kinds of conversations to exchange phone numbers and or agree to talk again.

And fourth, evangelization means *inviting* others to take whatever small steps they may be ready for: starting to pray again; being willing to read or share about spirituality; coming to a program, concert, or social event; or even attending Mass or a church service. And, by all means, we offer to come with them or meet them there. People are seldom willing to come to something all by themselves. As I mentioned before, there are literally thousands of non-practicing Christians out there who are not totally satisfied with being away from the church, but they will not make the first move to return on their own. But if someone invites them, they will respond. As one minister says, "There is power in the reaching out of the hand!"

So there you have it: this is what evangelization is basically about. It is a form of "relational evangelism"—not preaching necessarily, but using ordinary relational events to reach people with the Gospel of Jesus. I have had many occasions to teach these simple skills to Catholic men and women in parishes. I call it "How to share your faith without being obnoxious." At the end, people often say things like, "You know, I think I can do this!" Most of us are not called to be preachers or evangelists in the style of Peter and Paul. But we can "spread the good news" by our example of kindness, helpfulness, and generosity. I urge you, men, to follow the famous quote attributed to St. Francis of Assisi: "Preach the Gospel always; if necessary, use words."

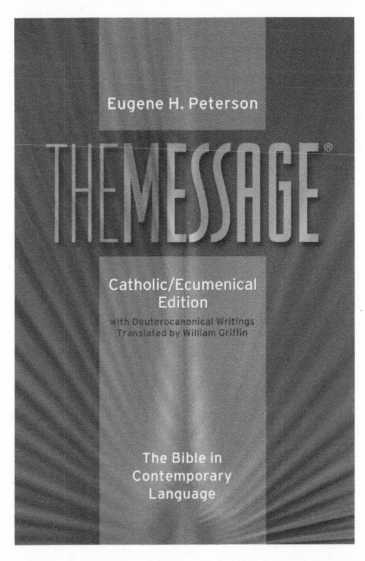

Books of Related Interest

INVITATION TO CATHOLICISM
INVITATION TO THE OLD TESTAMENT
INVITATION TO THE NEW TESTAMENT
by Alice Camille

Three separate but related books that offer clear, concise, and informative explanations of Catholicism and both the Old and New Testaments.

THE FORGIVENESS BOOK
by Alice Camille and Paul Boudreau

Perhaps the single best explanation of and guide to the Christian approach to forgiveness based on love.

THE CONFIRMED CATHOLIC'S COMPANION
by Mary Kathleen Glavich, SND

Full of facts, stories, prayers, quotes, places, and insights regarding Catholicism.

Books by Martin Pable, OFM Cap

CATHOLICS AND FUNDAMENTALISTS
Understanding and Response

PRAYER
A Practical Guide

RECLAIM THE FIRE
A Parish Guide to Evangelization

REMAINING CATHOLIC
Six Good Reasons for Staying in an Imperfect Church

AVAILABLE FROM ACTA PUBLICATIONS
actapublications.com • 800-397-2282